HOW TO MANGA

☑ W9-BNO-902

POCKET SIZED! with BEN DUNN

and DAVID HUTCHISON

With Additional text by ROBERT ACOSTA

Antarctic Press Presents: How to Draw Manga Pocket Manga Vol. 2, **June 2008**, is published by Antarctic Press, 7272 Wurzbach, Suite #204, San Antonio, Texas, 78240. FAX#: (210) 614-5029. Text © Ben Dunn, Robert Acosta & David Hutchison. Art © Ben Dunn & David Hutchison. All other material is ™ and © Antarctic Press. No similarity to any actual person(s) and/or place(s) is intended, and any such similarity is entirely coincidental. Nothing from this book may be reproduced without the express written consent of the authors, except for purposes of review or promotion. *"Wow, you made a verb out of 'Hogarth.'"* 2nd Printing. Printed and bound in Canada by Imprimerie Lebonton, Inc.

For more great "How to DRAW" merchandise, go to:

WWW.APMANGA.C

HOW TO DRAW MANGA

Drawing The Face

It is important to have a good idea where everything on the face rests in relation to the other features from both the front and the side. You may think that, since you are going to be drawing huge eyes and tiny mouths and noses, this is not important. On the contrary, it is even more critical to be aware of the proper location of the major facial features before you start to change them around. This will ensure that your facial proprtions maintain visual consistency.

Front View

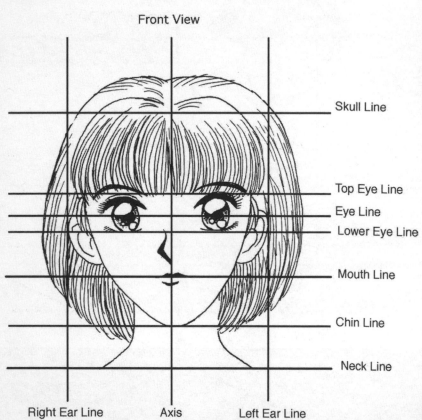

Skull Line

Top Eye Line

Eye Line

Lower Eye Line

Mouth Line

Chin Line

Neck Line

Right Ear Line   Axis   Left Ear Line

Drawing The Face

There are a lot of lines going across this head, as there were on the last one. These lines are to help you understand where objects on a face rest in relation to each other. For instance, the center of the eye is approximately aligned with the center of the ear. By understanding these proportions, we can see that even if you are drawing huge eyes and tiny ears, if the center of each lines up, you are creating a face that will be following the guidelines of a normal face.

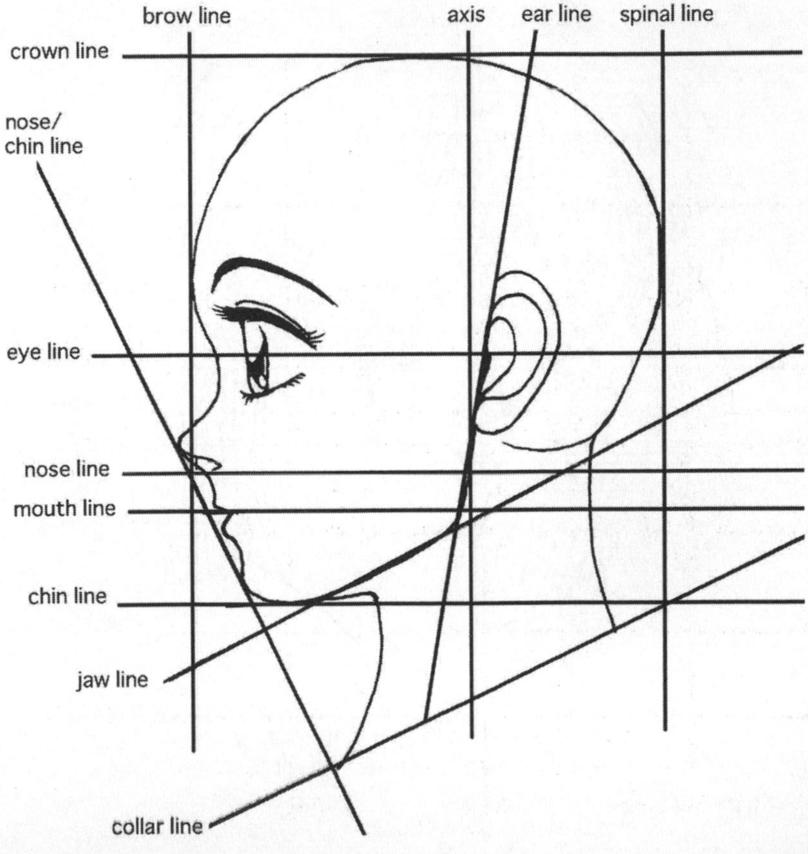

brow line
axis
ear line
spinal line
crown line
nose/ chin line
eye line
nose line
mouth line
chin line
jaw line
collar line

HOW TO DRAW MANGA

Gender Differences In Heads

There are obvious differences in facial structure and proportions between male and female faces and heads. In shoujo, you are free to reduce those differences as much as you want in the pursuit of creating bishounen, but it is best to understand what the differences in facial structure are before you start experimenting.

Female eyes are bigger with more lashes. They have a softer curve to their face, and petite noses, their mouths are smaller, and they have thin necks. They generally have more highlights in their hair.

HOW TO DRAW MANGA

Gender Differences In Heads

Males tend to have smaller eyes, sharper facial features, longer faces, slightly larger noses, bigger mouths, and thicker necks.

Remember, in shoujo, you are free to blend the features of men and women as much as you like.

Mouths

Referring back to the proportions drawing, we see that the mouth usually lies halfway between the tip of the chin and the bottom of the eyes. In shoujo, the mouth is often understated and almost invisible when closed. This can change quickly when the character becomes excited, and the mouth can become ridiculously large.

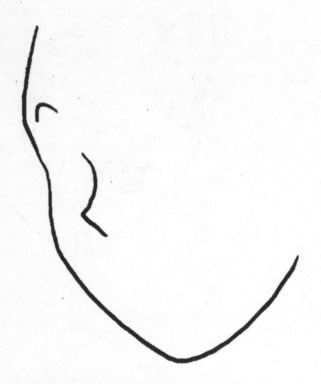

Here we have a basic face template to which we can add mouths. When you start expressing strong emotion, you enter a whole different arena, and face shape is pretty much up to you.

HOW TO DRAW MANGA

Mouths

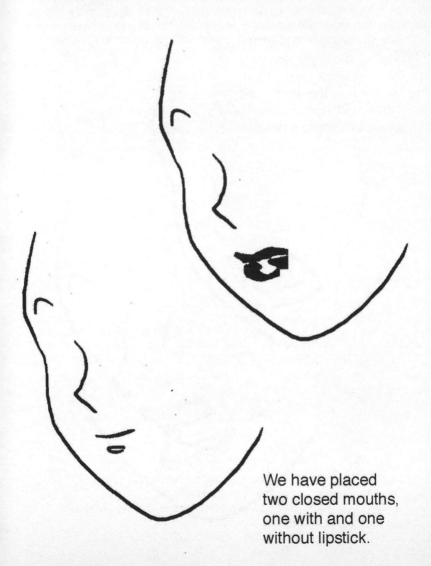

We have placed
two closed mouths,
one with and one
without lipstick.

Mouths

On this face, we have an open mouth yelling. Notice that it is not necessary to separate the individual teeth. Also, notice how the mouth opens down and the top of the mouth stays in the same position.

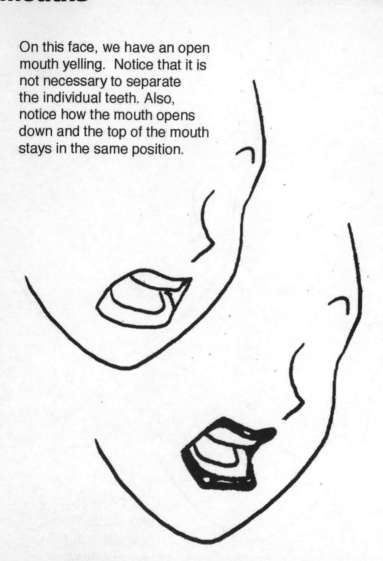

PRACTICE PAGE

Eyes

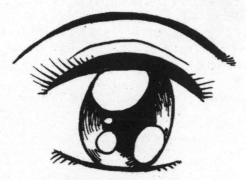

Here are two example eyes for quick reference.
First, notice that the eyebrow extends around the
pupil. Then, notice the light reflecting off of the iris.
This is especially common in shoujo, and the more
light that is reflected, the more intense the emotions
of the current scene are.

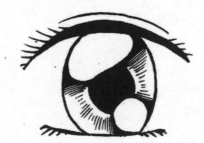

Note how these two eyes each use different styles of
iris. The top is a scratch method iris, with lines being
drawn around the pupil. The bottom is a radial iris, with
lines being drawn out from the pupil.

By playing with the shape of the eye, you can create a
wide range of emotions and effects.

Eyes

When you draw the eye, a smart way to begin is with a simple circle. Using that circle to build on, you can construct the entire eye, from highlights to eyelashes. An important thing to remember when you draw eyes is that the circle you start with will change in shape as the character's head turns and moves, like the example below.

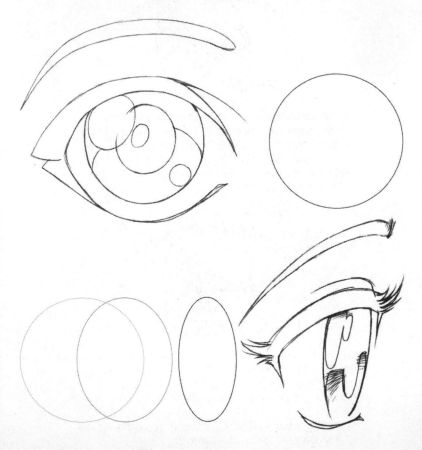

Eyes

First, you want to begin with the
outside shape of the eye, then
work your way inward, drawing
the line for the pupil.

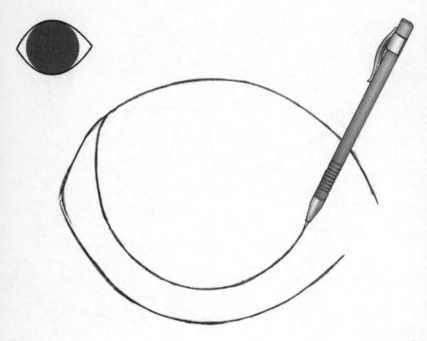

Eyes

Next, the circle for the iris should be drawn in the center of the pupil.

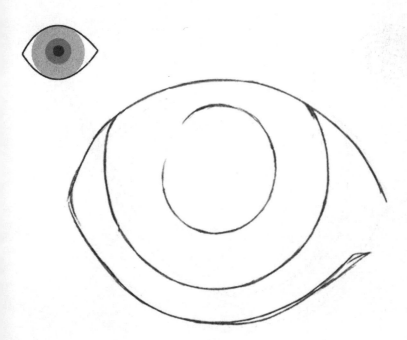

HOW TO DRAW MANGA

Eyes

Now it's time to lay out the high-lights. So what are highlights? Highlights are where the light is reflected off of a surface. A great trick to highlights is to draw a set of them that look good and use them every time you draw eyes, a reflective ball (if you can find one) can help you figure out highlights.

Eyes

Now that the eye and highlights are drawn, it's time for the extras. The eyebrow should typically follow the contour of the top line of the eye. When it comes to eyelashes, you should approach them as a single mass. The top eyelid lashes will be a larger mass than the lower eyelid lashes. Finally, draw in the shadows using the top lid to guide you.

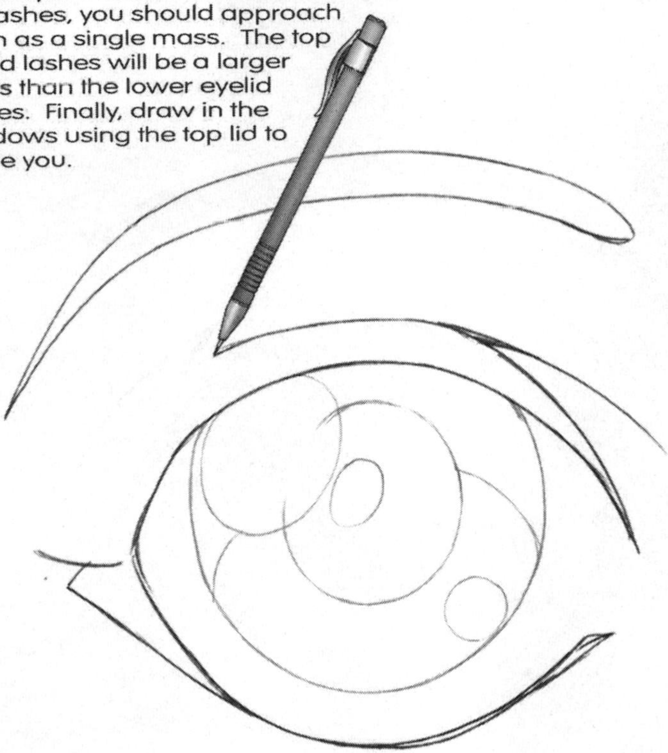

HOW TO DRAW MANGA

Eyes

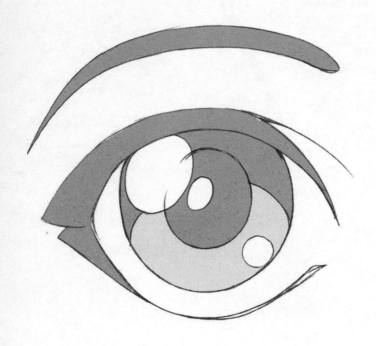

PRACTICE PAGE

HOW TO DRAW MANGA

Eyes

There are many ways to draw eyes, and the way you draw the eyes in manga is a strong indicator of the personality of your characters. Typically, rounded shapes tend to belong to the characters that are the heroes or heroines. Angles are used for the characters that are evil or whose motives are questionable or unknown.

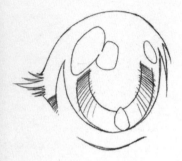

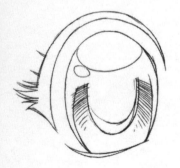

HOW TO DRAW MANGA

Eyes

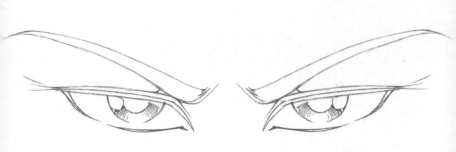

Eyes

When you're drawing your many characters, there will be times when you have to draw older characters. A good rule of thumb is the more lines you draw around a person's eyes, the older they will look. When you're drawing the wrinkles around the eyes, the lines should follow the contours of the outside of the eye. As you can see, the lines originate in the same places in the corners of the eyes and progressively droop downward.

HOW TO DRAW MANGA

Eyes

HOW TO DRAW MANGA

Eyes

PRACTICE PAGE

Eyes

When placing eyes on a face, be sure that the line of the eyebrow extends through to the line of the nose, even if you erase most of the nose. As your drawing nears completion, this guideline is a good idea when first placing the major facial features.

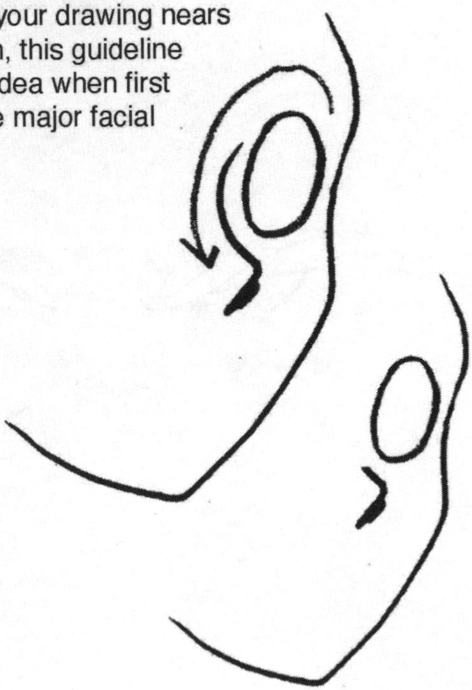

You can either place the eyes or the nose first, but remember either way you do it, their lines need to be in agreement.

HOW TO DRAW MANGA

Eyes

Here's a couple of different exam-ples of how the center guideline can be used to draw the eyes.

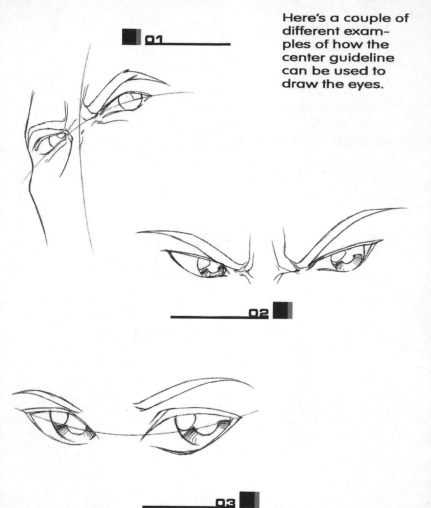

Eyes

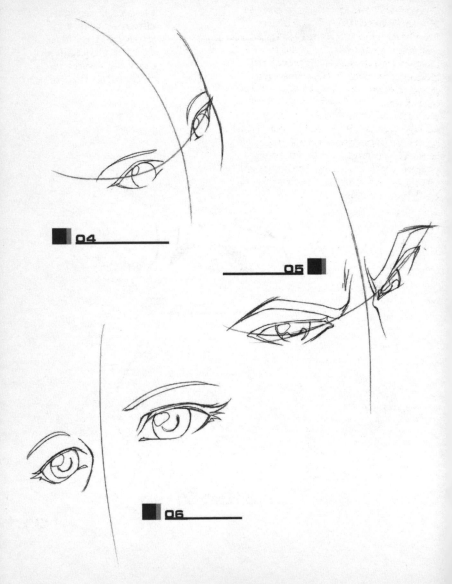

HOW TO DRAW MANGA

Breaking Down the Nose

Drawing the manga nose is an exercise in minimalism. Starting with a traditionally rendered nose, you can begin to break it down into basic separations. By stripping away all the other lines, leaving only the line for the bridge of the nose and the shadow underneath, we start to develop the beginnings of a manga nose. From this point, you can minimize the nose even more, depending on your tastes.

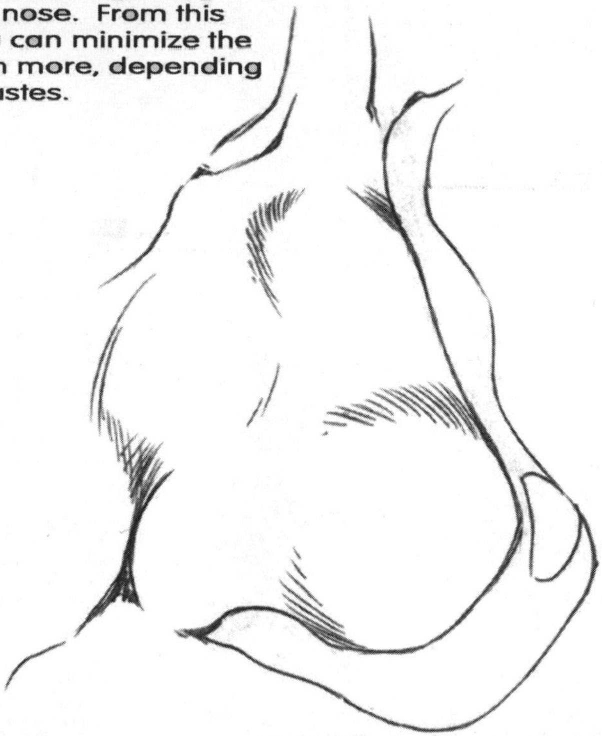

HOW TO DRAW MANGA
Breaking Down the Nose

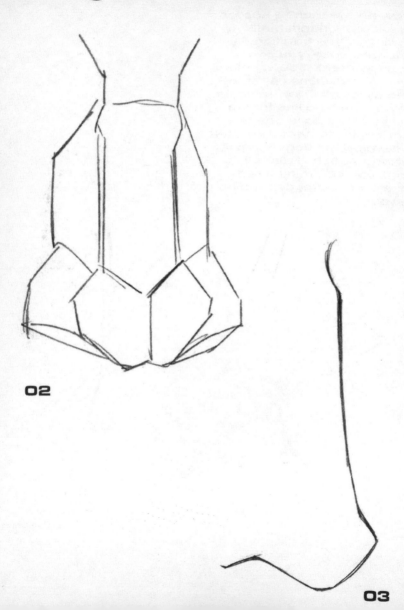

02

03

Breaking Down the Nose

04

05

PRACTICE PAGE

HOW TO DRAW MANGA

The Mouth

Drawing the guideline for the mouth is determined by splitting the difference between the bottom eye line and the bottom of the chin. That mouth line would be where the middle of the mouth is. We'll talk more about drawing the mouth later.

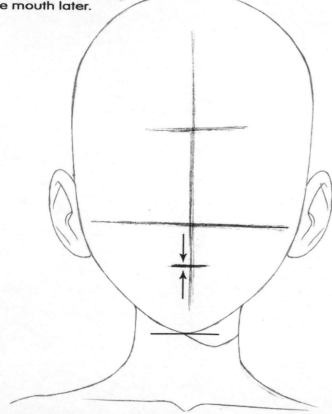

HOW TO DRAW MANGA

The Mouth

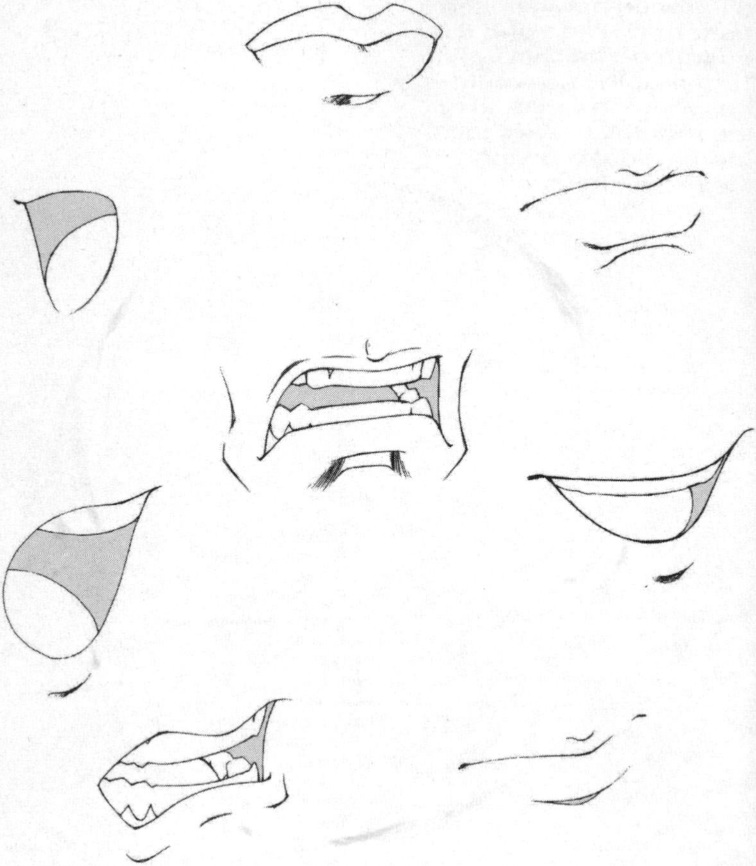

Eyes

Because of the simple structure of the manga style face, there are many, many ways to express emotion.

Here are a few examples of the more common emotions on very simple faces. The key characteristics to look for are the shape and placement of the mouth and the shape and placement of the eyebrows

apologetic

Eyes

Eyebrows and eyelids tilted upwards give off a negative emotion on the face of a character.

sad

shocked or surprised

HOW TO DRAW MANGA

Eyes

These emotions all have downward-curving eyebrows. This is usually a sign of negative emotion like anger or sadistic glee.

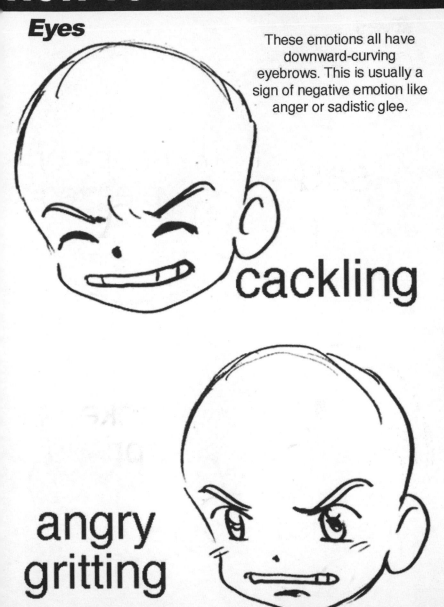

cackling

angry gritting

HOW TO DRAW MANGA

Eyes

These examples demonstrate positive emotions.

happy or pleased

very happy or excited

Eyes

The tilted eyebrows combined with a smiling mouth complete the effect.

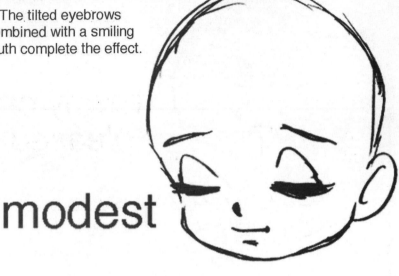

modest

wily

HOW TO DRAW MANGA

Expressions

Blush

WHEN NORMAL BLUSHING SIMPLY ISN'T ENOUGH, YOU CAN MAKE A CHARACTER CUTER BY ADDING BLUSH CIRCLES. MORE OFTEN THAN NOT, THESE CIRCLES ARE SEEN ON YOUNGER CHARACTERS. SOMETIMES THEY ARE USED AS A PART OF THE CHARACTER DESIGN.

Expressions

Veins

THIS TYPE OF VEIN IS OFTEN USED TO DENOTE AN ANNOYED CHARACTER. TYPICALLY A COMICAL ELEMENT, THEY ARE USED BOTH ON AND OFF OF THE BODY. YOU DON'T JUST HAVE TO USE THESE ON THE FOREHEAD.

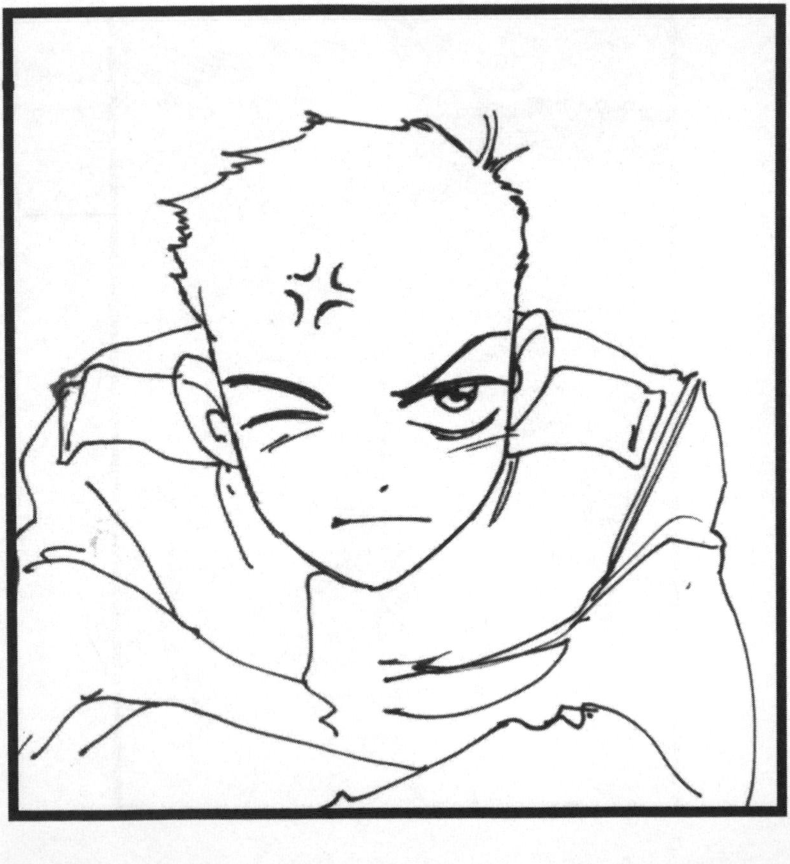

Expressions

Steam

THIS IS A COMMON DEVICE IN BOTH AMERICAN AND JAPANESE COMICS. STEAM HAS ANY NUMBER OF USES, SOME OF WHICH WILL BE COVERED LATER.

HOW TO DRAW MANGA

Expressions

Swirls

THESE TYPES OF SWIRLS ARE OFTEN USED TO SHOW THAT SOMETHING IS WRONG INSIDE THE CHARACTER, EITHER MENTALLY OR PHYSICALLY.

HOW TO DRAW MANGA

Expressions

Sparks

GENERALLY, SPARKS ARE USED TO SHOW RECOGNITION OR SUDDEN AWARENESS OF A SITUATION.

HOW TO DRAW MANGA

Expressions

Tears

TEARS OF THE TYPE SEEN BELOW ARE USED FOR MORE COMICAL SITUATIONS. YOU DON'T USUALLY SEE THIS TYPE IN SERIOUS STORIES.

HOW TO DRAW MANGA

Expressions

NOW LET'S TAKE A LOOK AT HOW SOME OF THESE IDEAS CAN BE COMBINED. HERE ARE SOME EXAMPLES OF OVERLAPPING DEVICES USED IN VARIOUS SITUATIONS.

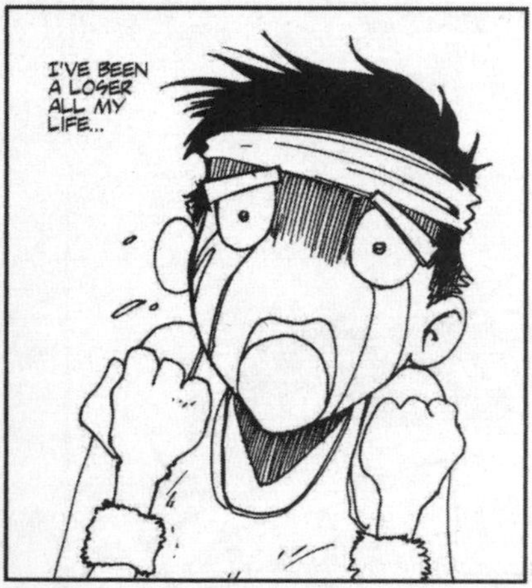
I'VE BEEN A LOSER ALL MY LIFE...

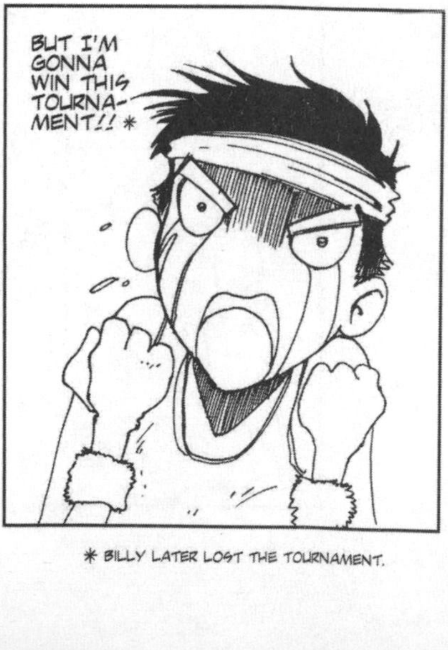
BUT I'M GONNA WIN THIS TOURNAMENT!! *

IN THIS INSTANCE, WE'LL GO BACK TO OUR TEAR EXAMPLE. I JUST WANTED TO POINT OUT THAT WITH A SIMPLE SWITCH OF THE EYEBROWS, WE CAN MAKE OUR CHARACTER'S PERSONALITY COMPLETELY CHANGE FROM TOTALLY BROKEN TO BOUND AND DETERMINED.

* BILLY LATER LOST THE TOURNAMENT.

HOW TO DRAW MANGA

Expressions

THE SAME IS TRUE IN THIS EXAMPLE.

HOW TO DRAW MANGA

Expressions

HERE ARE SOME OTHER SITUATIONS YOU COULD PUT YOUR CHARACTERS IN:

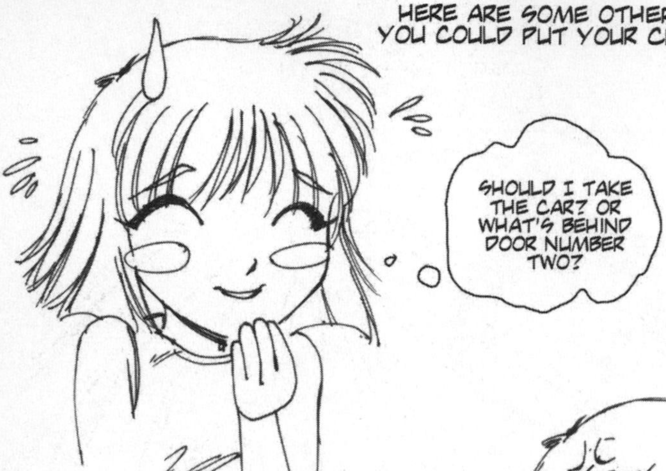
SHOULD I TAKE THE CAR? OR WHAT'S BEHIND DOOR NUMBER TWO?

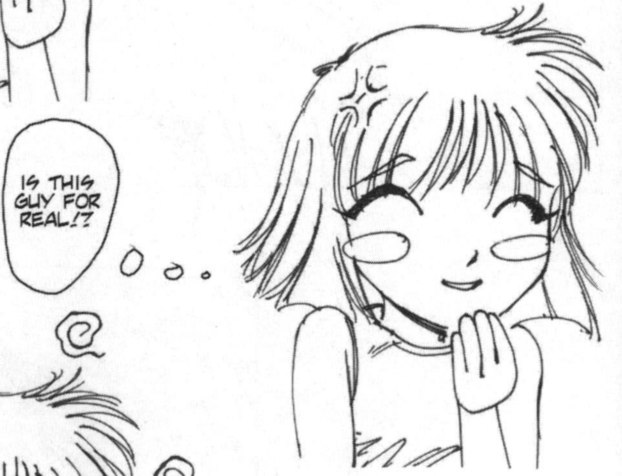
IS THIS GUY FOR REAL!?

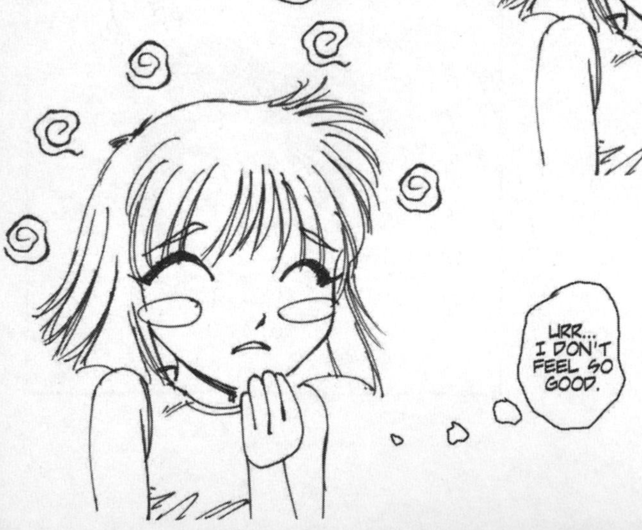
URR... I DON'T FEEL SO GOOD.

Expressions

HERE IS A MORE TRADITIONAL USE FOR TEARS. MANGA CHARACTERS TEND TO TEAR UP A LOT FROM EMOTION AND STRESS.

I DON'T BELIEVE IT!

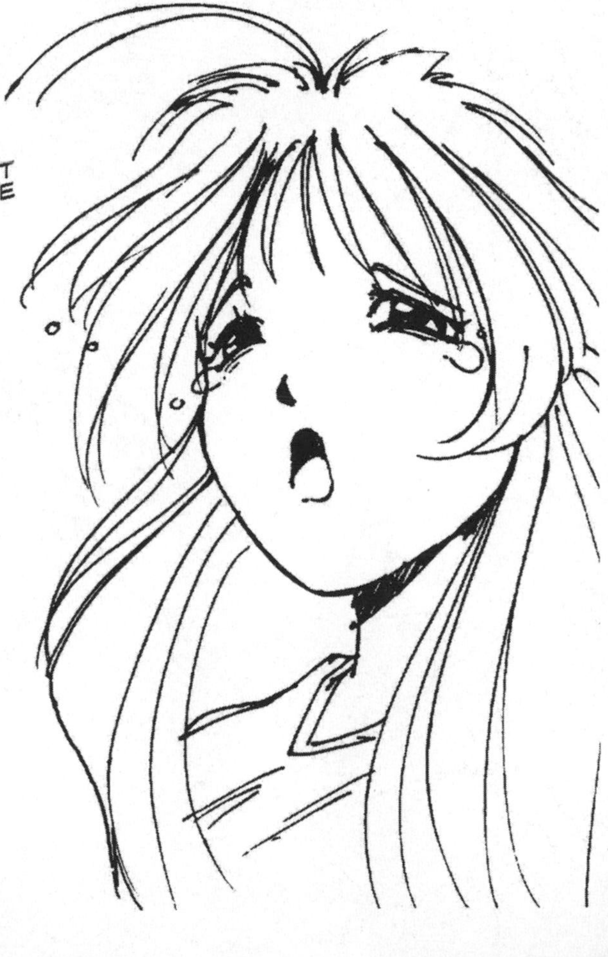

SEARCH YOUR FEELINGS... YOU KNOW IT TO BE TRUE!

Expressions

WHEN A CHARACTER COMES TO A REALIZATON OR UNDERSTANDING, OR WHEN THEY ARE SURPRISED OR OTHERWISE CAUGHT OFF GUARD, YOU WILL USUALLY SEE SOME TYPE OF SPARK EFFECT TO INDICATE IT VISUALLY.

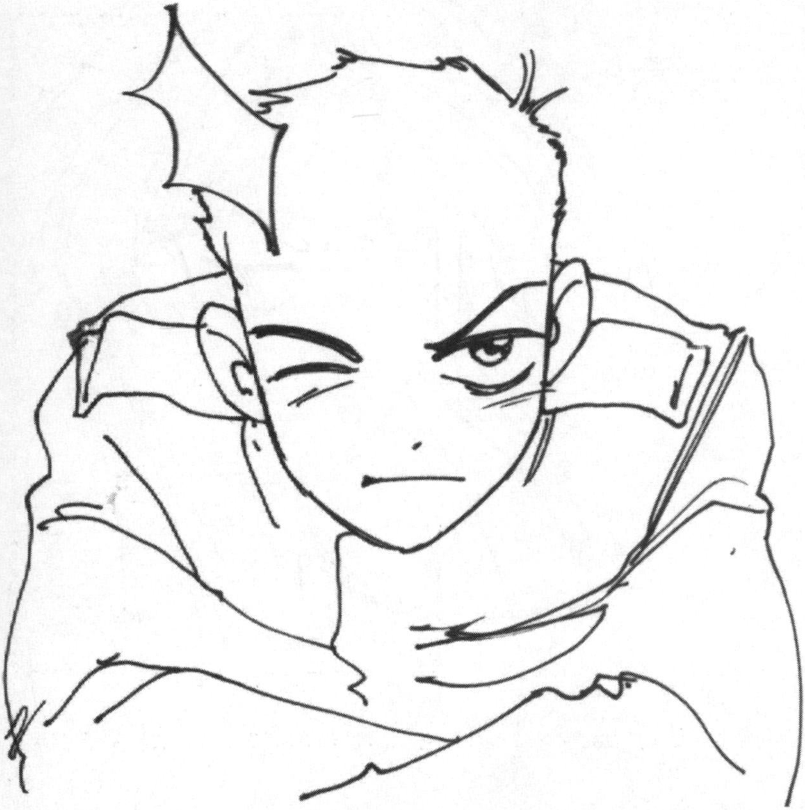

HOW TO DRAW MANGA

Expressions

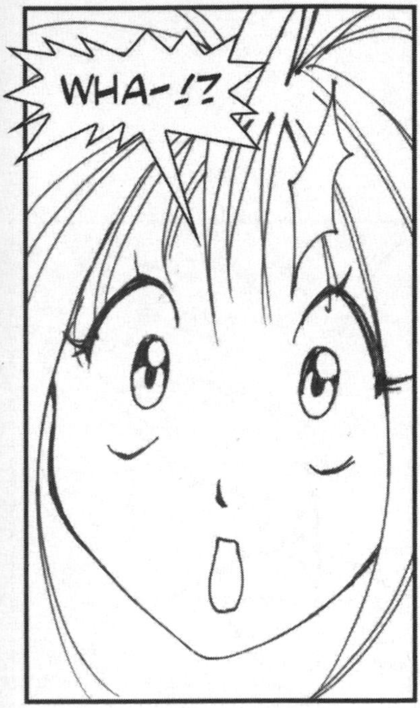
WHA-!?

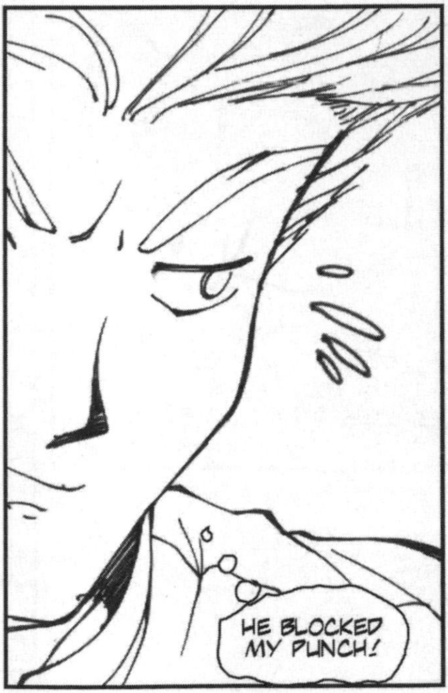
HE BLOCKED MY PUNCH!

IN THESE TWO EXAMPLES, THE MOOD OF THE SITUATION CAN BE MANIPULATED BY EXCHANGING THE REACTIONS OF THE CHARACTERS AND REWRITING THE DIALOGUE.

Expressions

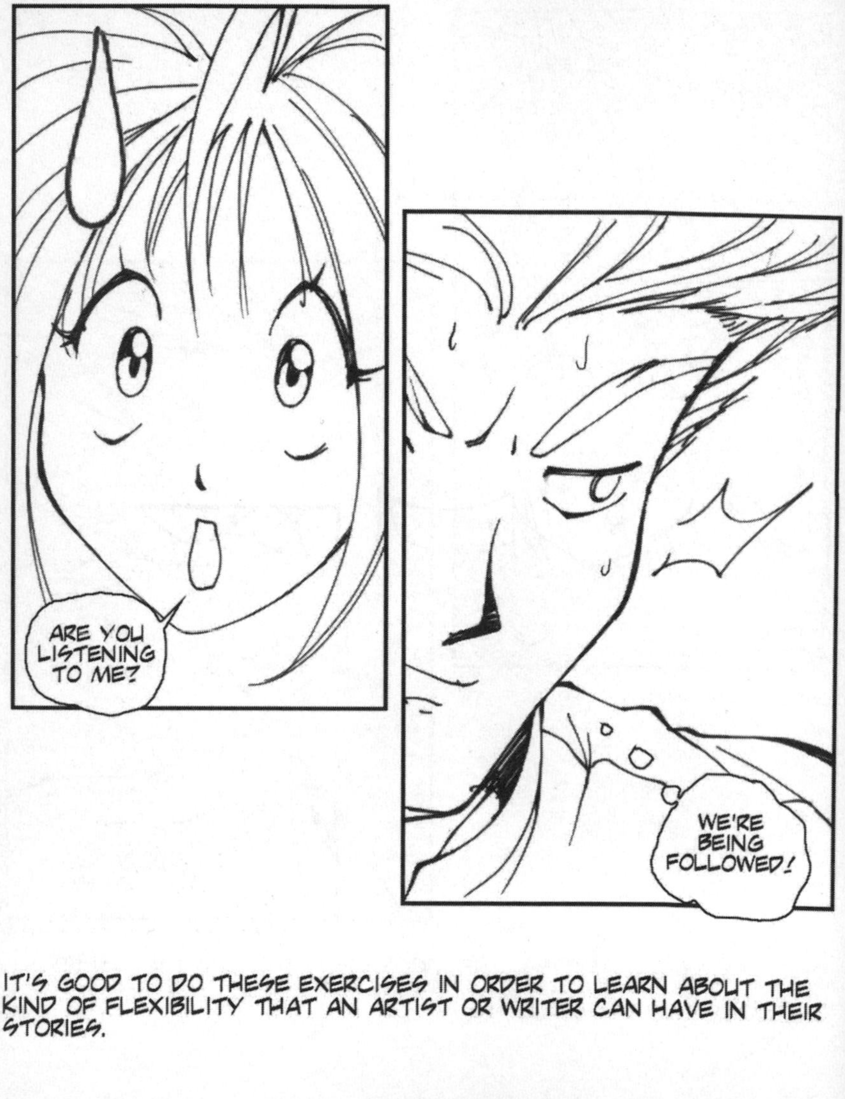
ARE YOU LISTENING TO ME?
WE'RE BEING FOLLOWED!

IT'S GOOD TO DO THESE EXERCISES IN ORDER TO LEARN ABOUT THE KIND OF FLEXIBILITY THAT AN ARTIST OR WRITER CAN HAVE IN THEIR STORIES.

HOW TO DRAW MANGA

Expressions

I THINK BLUSH IS USED FAR TOO MUCH IN MANGA-INSPIRED ARTWORK. IT IS NOT OFTEN USED AS IT SHOULD BE, TO INDICATE A BLUSH, BUT AS A FACIAL DETAIL. MANY TIMES, THE ARTIST WILL USE LINES TO SHOW THE PLANE OF THE NOSE AND CHEEKS, AND IT CAN BE DIFFICULT TO TELL THE DIFFERENCE IF YOU AREN'T CAREFUL.

Expressions

THERE ARE A COUPLE OF DETAILS IN THIS EXAMPLE THAT I WANT TO REFER TO, BUT FOR NOW I JUST WANT TO MENTION THE CHEEK LINES ON THE FACE. THESE ARE JUST SKETCHY INDICATIONS OF THE SURFACE OF THE CHEEKS.

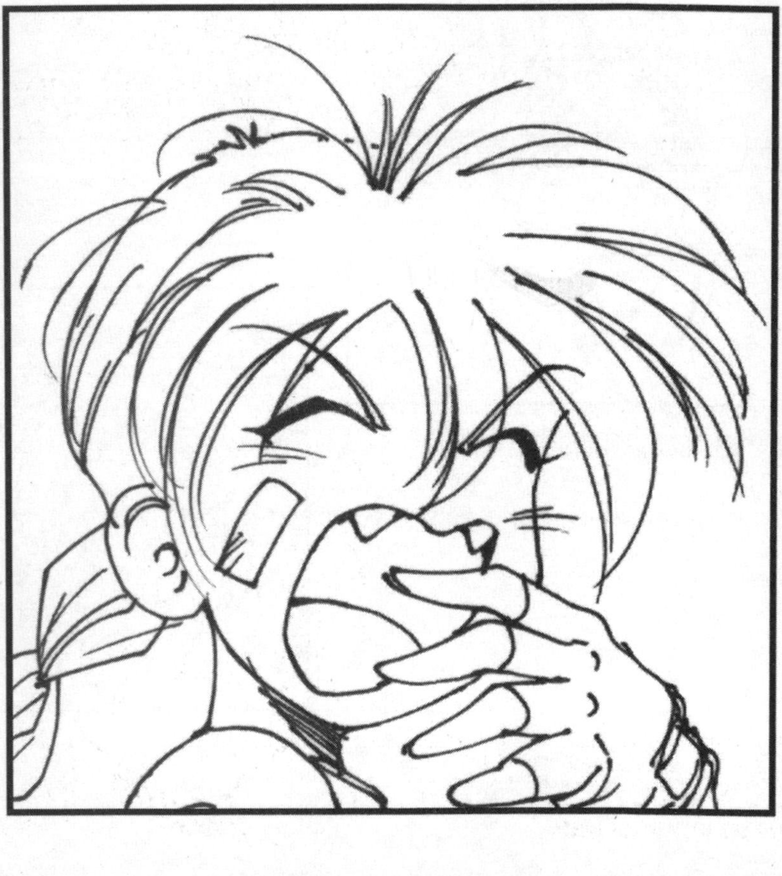

Expressions

HERE'S SOMETHING YOU CAN DO TO SHOW YOUR CHARACTER'S FACE FROM TWO DIFFERENT POINTS OF VIEW.

IN THIS CASE, YOU CAN DRAW A NORMAL FRONT VIEW. ONCE YOU'VE DRAWN THE OUTER FORM, ALL YOU NEED TO DO IS ADJUST FACIAL RELATIONS.

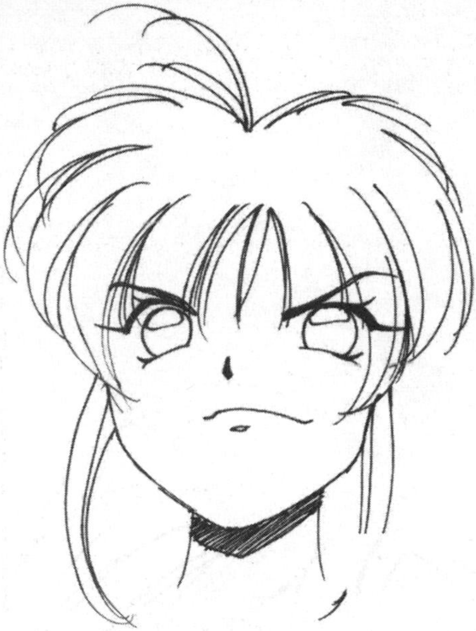

HERE, THE CHARACTER'S FACE IS SLIGHTLY UPTURNED. SIMPLY MOVE ALL OF THE FACIAL ELEMENTS CLOSER TO THE FOREHEAD.

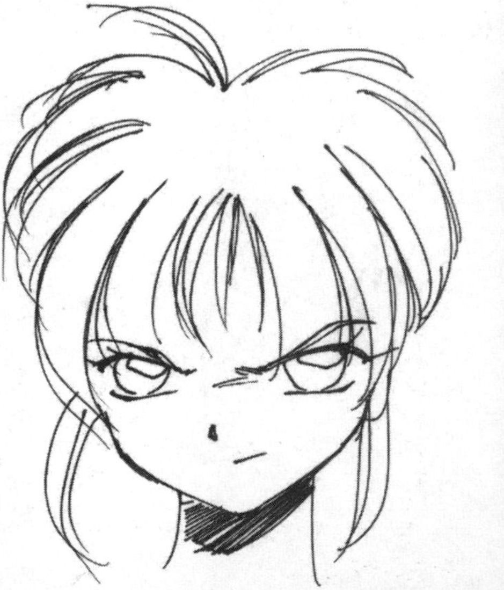

IN THIS SHOT, DRAW THE FACIAL ELEMENTS CLOSER TO THE BOTTOM OF THE HEAD TO MAKE THE CHARACTER'S HEAD SEEM TO BE DOWNTURNED.

PRACTICE PAGE

HOW TO DRAW MANGA

Applying Hair

We have talked a great deal about different hairstyles,
heads, and rotation, so next we need to combine them
and talk about applying hair to your character's head.

First, draw a hairline on your character's head. This will act as a guide to placing
the hairstyle you have selected.

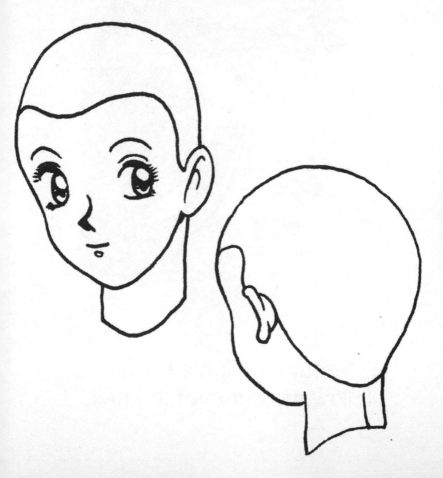

HOW TO DRAW MANGA

Applying Hair

Second, decide on your hairstyle.

* Your highlights should
follow the curve of the hair.

Applying Hair

Third, draw the basic shape of the hairstyle.

* Feathering the edge of
the sheen gives the
illusion of strands of hair.

HOW TO DRAW MANGA

Applying Hair

Fourth, start drawing hair. Be sure to use thin lines so that you don't get fat hair.

* Separating the edges of the hair also gives the impression of individual strands.

PRACTICE PAGE

Body Types

There are as many different body types as there are people, but in shoujo and manga in general, there are a number of body types that appear fairly frequently. The two most frequent shoujo types are adolescent-like in shape.

Adolescent Female

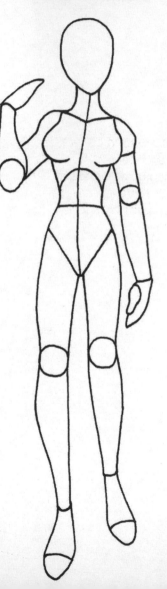

Most shoujo characters are adolescents or at least depicted that way. Hips on women are not very pronounced and breasts tend toward the smaller side.

Body Types

Adolescent Male

Males tend to be slender, tall, and not overly muscular, as opposed to the way they are often seen in shounen manga.

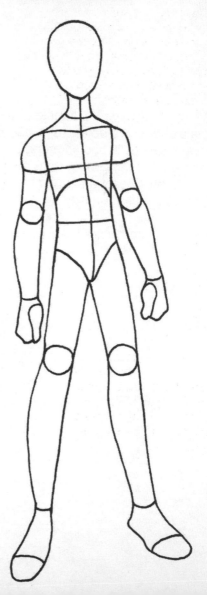

Body Types

Adult Female

Averge body type adult male and female characters do make frequent appearances in shoujo manga, usually in supporting roles. Parents, teachers, and any number of outside adult influences share these body types.

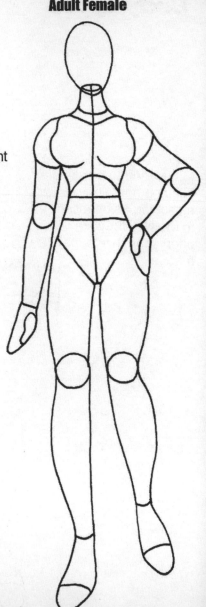

Body Types   **Adult Male**

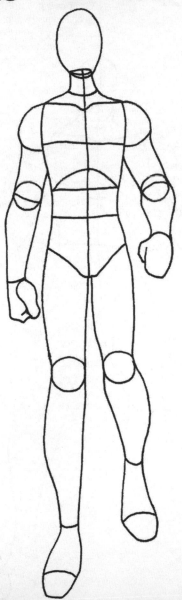

Body Types

Chances are pretty good that a muscle-bound character will pop up at some point. This body type is common among bullies, gym teachers, the heads of sports clubs, and possibly annoying older brothers.

Muscular Male

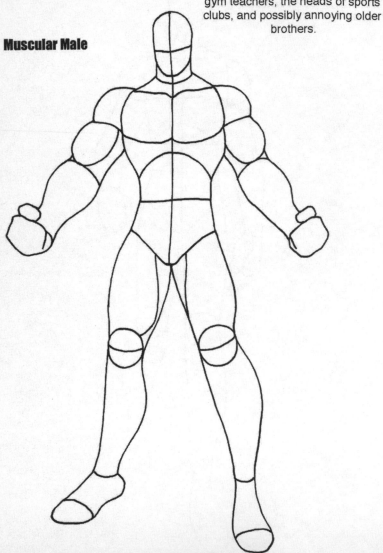

Body Types

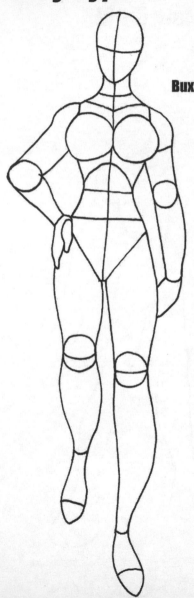

Buxom Female

The buxom female is another body type usually found in antagonists. Anyone from an older woman distracting your character's romantic interest to an evil temptress in a magical girl story can have this body type.

Body Types

Male Child

If the characters in your story are really young, you will want to use the child body type.

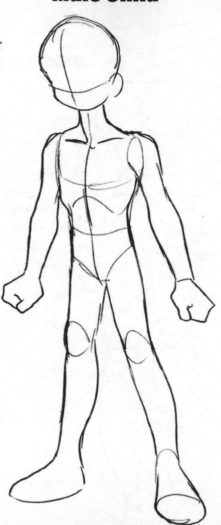

HOW TO DRAW MANGA

Body Types

Female Child

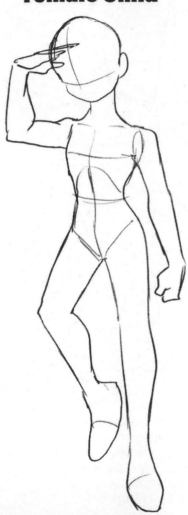

The key to drawing this body type is that by enlarging the head, you can make a figure appear to be younger in age.

Body Types

Chibi

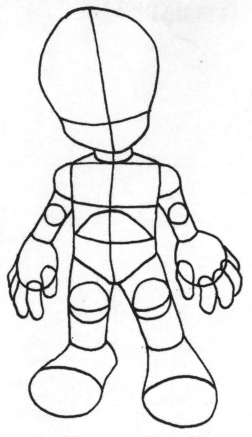

The chibi, or super deformed body type, is a visual tool common to all manga, shoujo or shounen. It is used in a variety of ways, but the figure usually has a very small body and a very large head.

PRACTICE PAGE

Hands and Feet

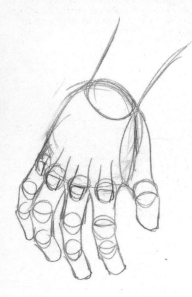

Looking at these drawings makes the hand look very complicated. The key to drawing the hand well is properly understanding the anatomy.

But if you don't want to study anatomy (which you really ought to), here's an easy way to approach drawing them.

HOW TO DRAW MANGA

Hands and Feet

Begin by drawing a circle for the palm of the hand. Look at your own hand for the placement of the lines that will later become the fingers. Then draw an oval to represent the thick part of the palm where the thumb connects. Use small circles to place the knuckles and cylinders for the fingers. After you've constructed the hand, you can then start rendering, use your own hand for a model.

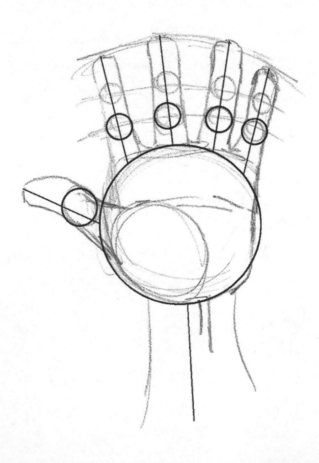

HOW TO DRAW MANGA
Hands and Feet

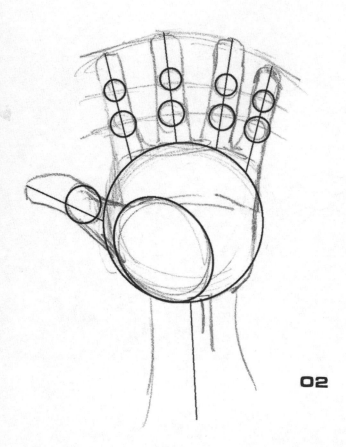

02

HOW TO DRAW MANGA

Hands and Feet

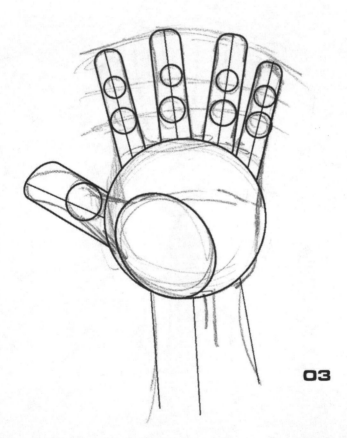

03

HOW TO DRAW MANGA

Hands and Feet

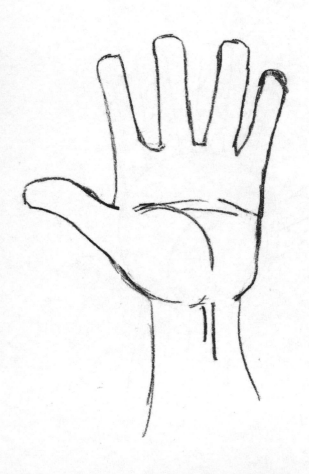

PRACTICE PAGE

HOW TO DRAW MANGA

Hands and Feet

When you're drawing the hand in different poses, the same principles apply. The difference is the use and understanding of cylinders becomes more important. As you can see below, the cylinders used for the fingers and forearm are drawn in perspective. Drawing the fingers individually using this approach will help you get the pose right and add the illusion of depth.

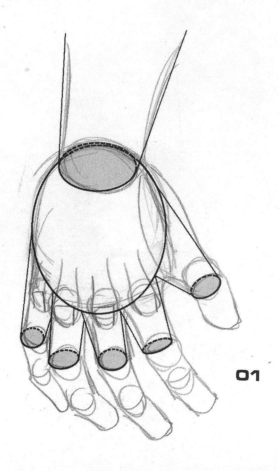

01

HOW TO DRAW MANGA

Hands and Feet

When you're drawing the hand in different poses, the same principles apply. The difference is the use and understanding of cylinders becomes more important. As you can see below, the cylinders used for the fingers and forearm are drawn in perspective. Drawing the fingers individually using this approach will help you get the pose right and add the illusion of depth.

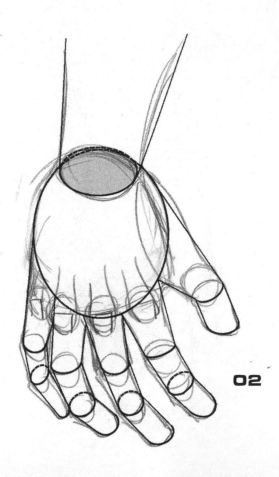

02

HOW TO DRAW MANGA

Hands and Feet

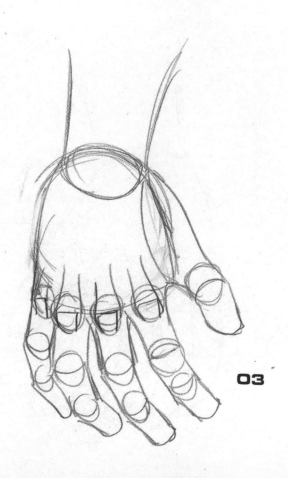

03

HOW TO DRAW MANGA

Hands and Feet

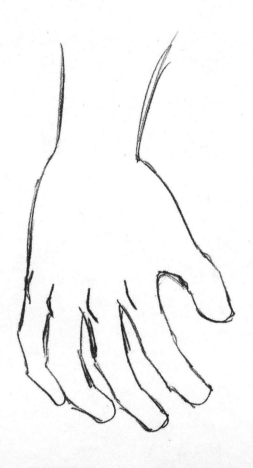

PRACTICE PAGE

Hands and Feet

Once you are able to understand how the hand and fingers work, you'll be able to apply that understanding to drawing the rest of the arm. Pose in a mirror or have someone pose for you, and take pictures in the pose you're trying to draw.

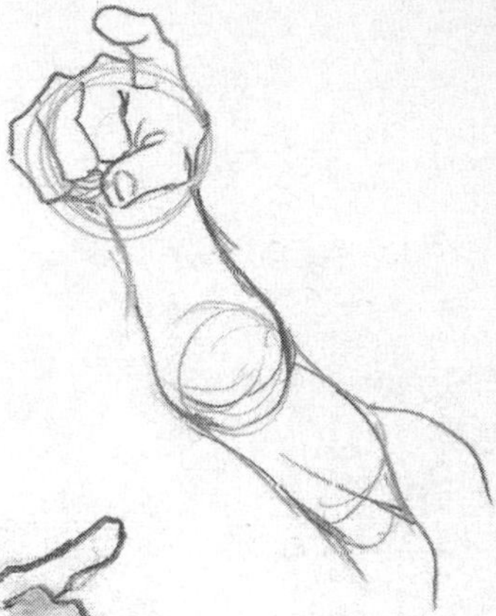

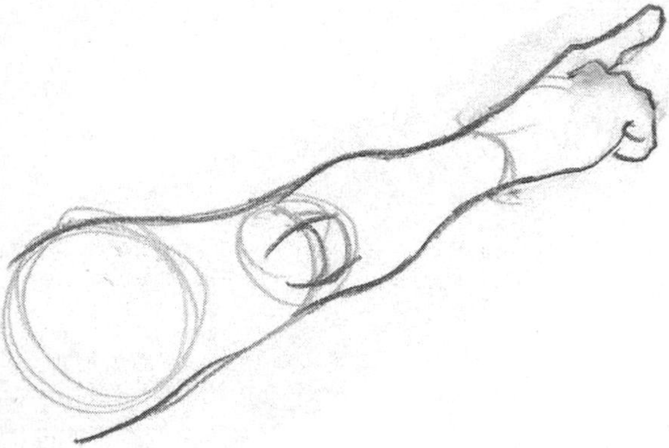

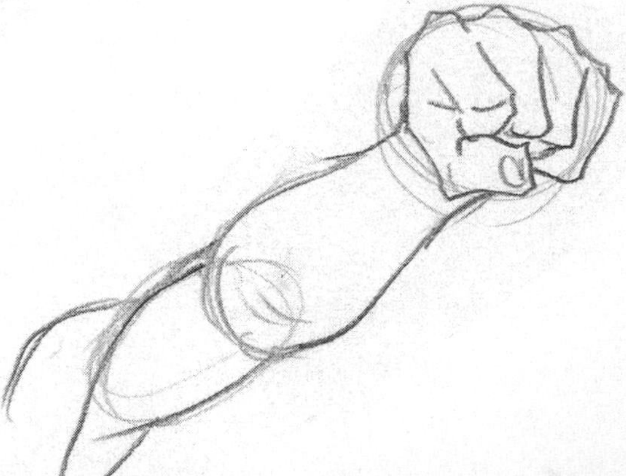

HOW TO DRAW MANGA
Hands and Feet

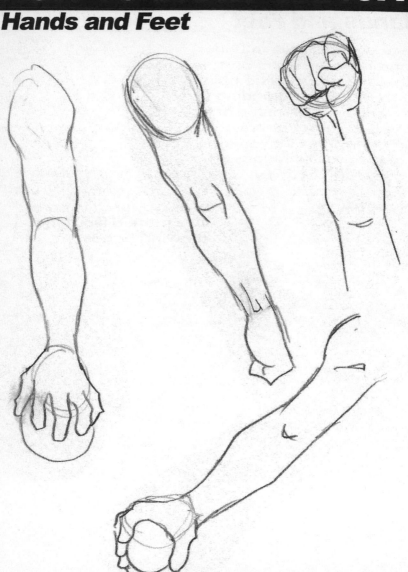

Hands and Feet

Feet may look simple, but once you get down to it, they tend to be a little more difficult than drawing hands.

From the bottom of the foot, they are much simpler than hands, but when you look at them the way they are normally seen, the complexity shows.

Hands and Feet

Feet generally can be broken down to two circles: a large circle for the "ball" of the foot and a circle about 1/3 smaller for the heel. Then you draw five circles for the toes, each one getting progressively smaller than the last. Then, you connect the front and back of the foot by drawing the arch and outside of the foot. Like I said before, this is probably the easiest pose the foot could be in, but it is the least common.

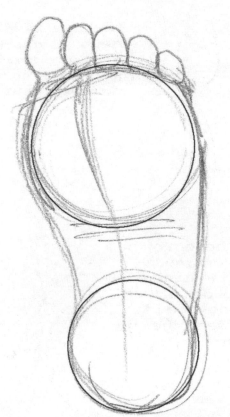

01

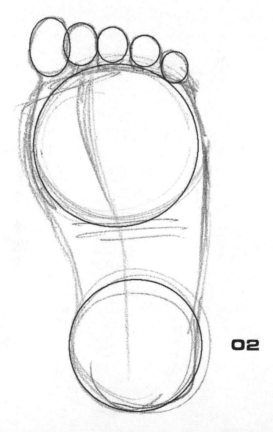

02

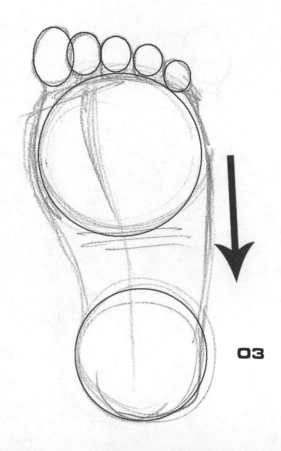

03

PRACTICE PAGE

HOW TO DRAW MANGA

Hands and Feet

Here's the foot like you'd typically see it. Notice the circles for the ball and heel are still there, but they're drawn in perspective to reflect the pose. The new addition is the circle drawn in for the ankle. This will help you figure out the connection for the rest of the leg. All the steps remain the same as in the last example except the toes. The toes will look more like cylinders, so approach drawing them that way.

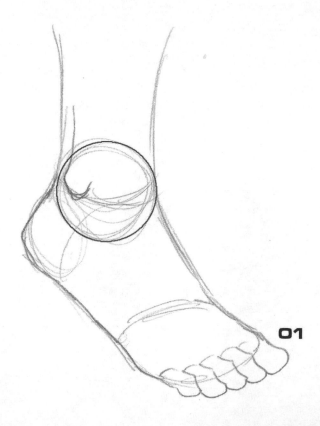

01

HOW TO DRAW MANGA

Hands and Feet

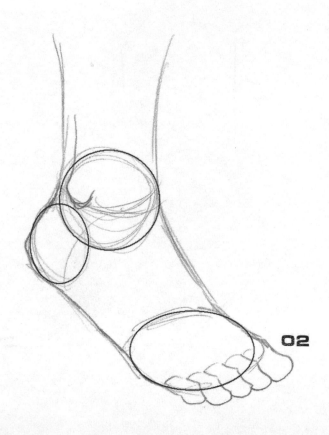

02

HOW TO DRAW MANGA
Hands and Feet

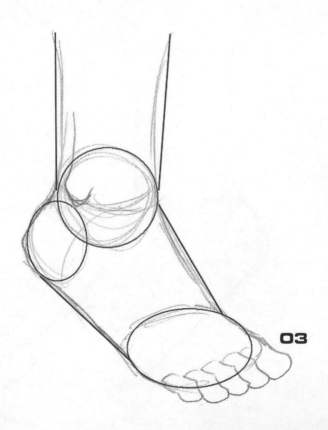

03

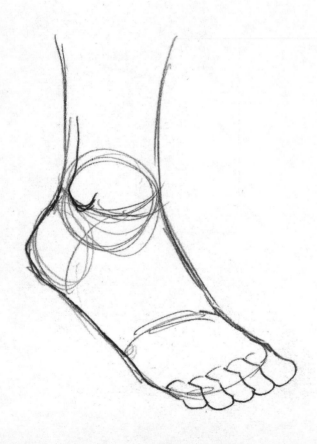

PRACTICE PAGE

Hands and Feet

Drawing the foot from the rear gets even more complicated due to the fact that the Achilles tendon is smack in the middle of the body part. When you break it down, all it is is a pair of triangles that touch at their tips. It's probably gonna be tough to look at your own foot from this angle, so get someone to pose for you or take a picture.

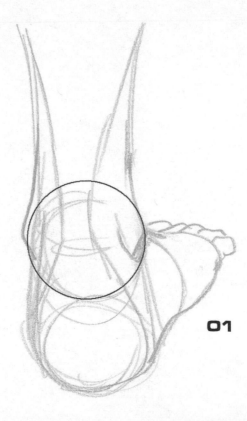

01

HOW TO DRAW MANGA

Hands and Feet

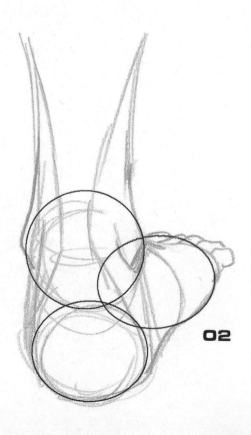

02

Hands and Feet

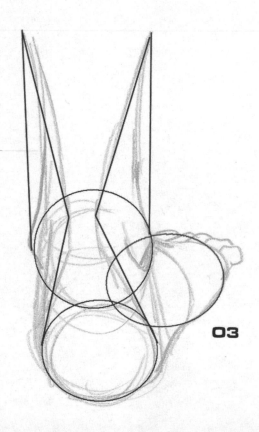

03

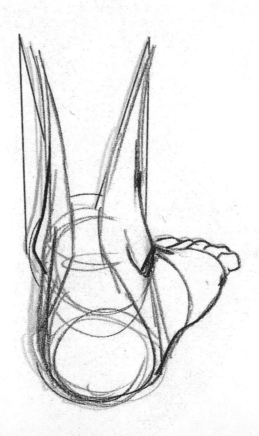

PRACTICE PAGE

Hands and Feet

Here's the feet and legs in action. When you're laying out the figure, the feet will generally be small ovals at the ends of the legs, but there will be times when it'll be necessary to draw in those little piggies. So, like the saying says, "there's no time like the present" to start understanding how to draw feet without the socks or shoes. Understanding now will make y drawing skill that much stronge

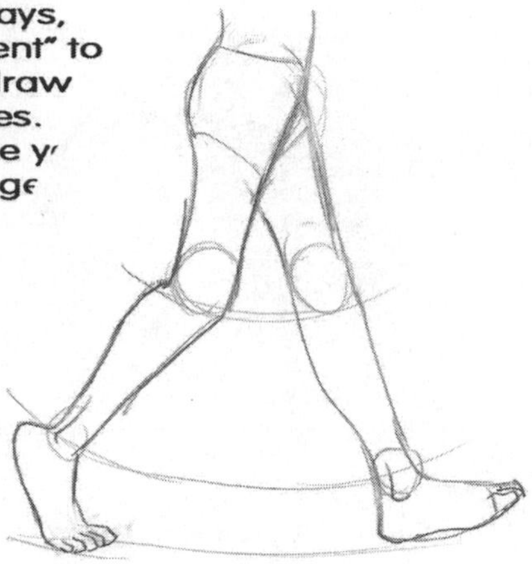

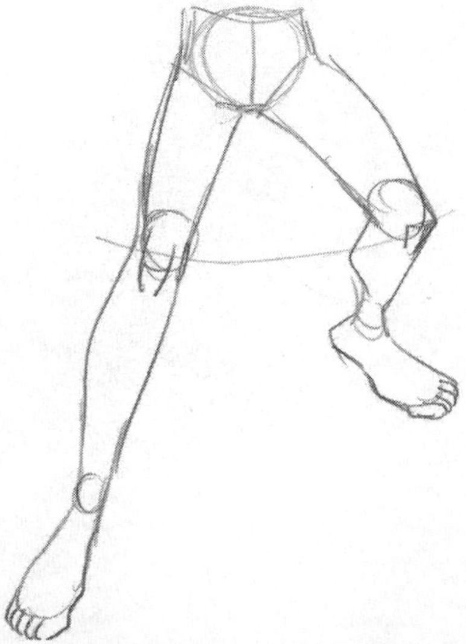

HOW TO DRAW MANGA
Hands and Feet

Articulation

You will hear the term "points of articulation" used frequently in this book and in many other situations, especially when discussing figures in movement.
A point of articulation is the point that controls movement of a portion of the body. It is important to know where the articulation points are and how they behave in order to draw characters with realistic and believable movement.

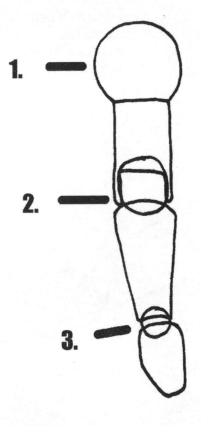

1.

2.

3.

In this simple drawing of an arm, the points of articulation are marked with circles. This means that you have three places you can determine the pose of the arm at.

Articulation

Along with knowing where the points of articulation are, it is a good idea to know how they behave. Luckily, we have our own bodies to use as reference.

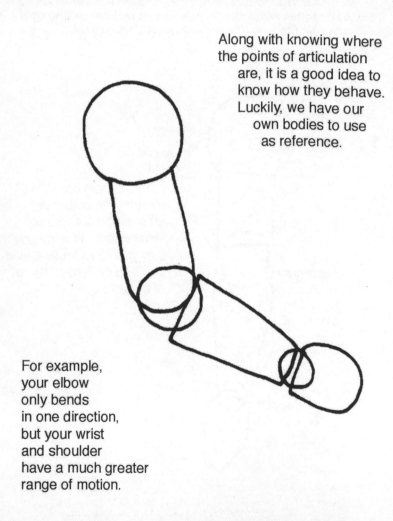

For example, your elbow only bends in one direction, but your wrist and shoulder have a much greater range of motion.

HOW TO DRAW MANGA

Articulation

So let us get into articulation a bit more. On this model, you will see more points of articulation. The human body has tons of them; you have 18 on each arm alone. When setting up your figures, you need to consider the big ones and work your way down to the smaller ones.

Articulation

We've already touched on the arms. The other three major areas are the head, torso, and legs. Getting these three areas right in your basic sketch is key.

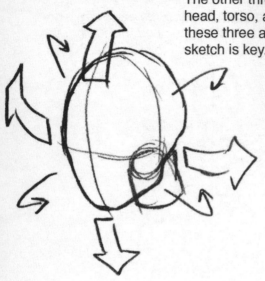

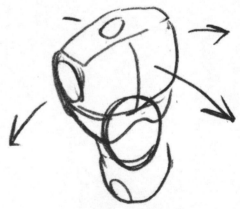

Articulation

Once you've finished this, you can start
to add details to your figure, and that is
when you consider the other points of
articulation, like the fingers and toes.

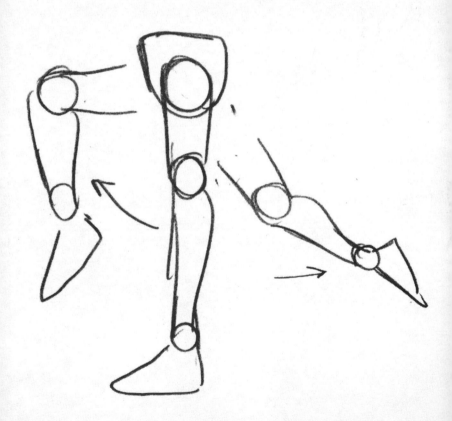

PRACTICE PAGE

HOW TO DRAW MANGA

Drawing The Figure

The main character of most Shonen manga and usually a big player in many Shoujo is the average male. Modest of build and height, this body type is one that you will be hard pressed to avoid using. Even if the style you choose to draw in is slightly different, the proportions on your average male character will follow this basic form!

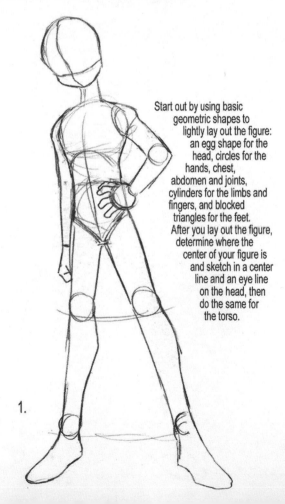

Start out by using basic geometric shapes to lightly lay out the figure: an egg shape for the head, circles for the hands, chest, abdomen and joints, cylinders for the limbs and fingers, and blocked triangles for the feet. After you lay out the figure, determine where the center of your figure is and sketch in a center line and an eye line on the head, then do the same for the torso.

1.

Drawing The Figure

2.

Drawing The Figure

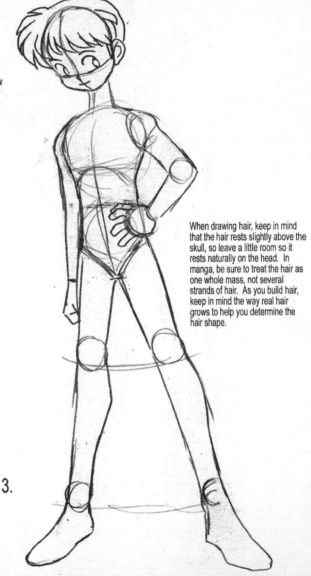

Using the guide-lines that you drew on the head, draw in eyes, the ear, nose, and mouth.

When drawing hair, keep in mind that the hair rests slightly above the skull, so leave a little room so it rests naturally on the head. In manga, be sure to treat the hair as one whole mass, not several strands of hair. As you build hair, keep in mind the way real hair grows to help you determine the hair shape.

3.

Drawing The Figure

Here's why you were supposed to draw lightly— now we get to add the costume. Remember, clothes don't fit right up against the body (unless you're wearing spandex or a body stocking) Allow a bit of room between the body and clothing. Use the layout figure as a guide. A good idea is to take a look at yourself in a mirror wearing something similar to your character's clothes, and standing in the same pose to get the folds, wrinkles, and details right.

4.

Drawing The Figure

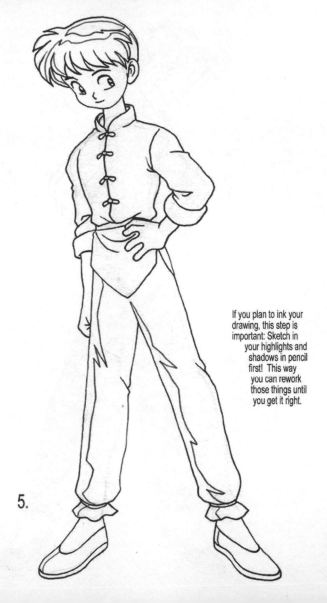

If you plan to ink your drawing, this step is important: Sketch in your highlights and shadows in pencil first! This way you can rework those things until you get it right.

5.

HOW TO DRAW MANGA

Drawing The Figure

You've got your illustration perfect. Now you ink it in! This last step is where you can add textures, freckles, or things that you think up on the fly, and you're done.

6.

PRACTICE PAGE

There are distinct differences between the male and female form, although in manga today, especially shoujo manga, those differences are intentionally minimized or completely disregarded.

The two major areas of difference between male and female are the chest and the hips. On males, the chest is larger and more barrel-shaped. In comparison, the female chest is more oval and tapers down.

← The main difference is this line. →

Male Female

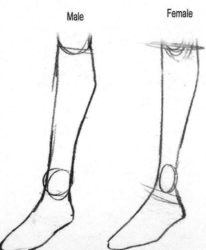

HOW TO DRAW MANGA

Drawing The Figure

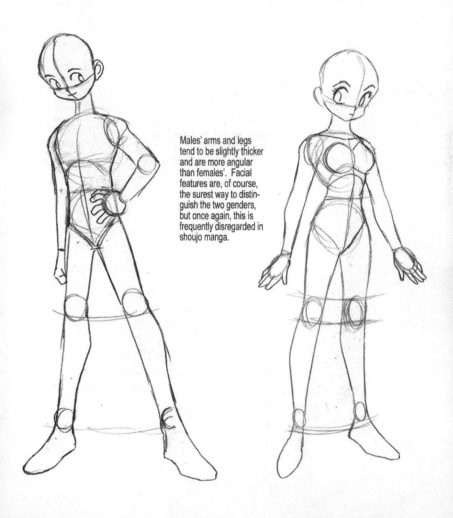

Males' arms and legs tend to be slightly thicker and are more angular than females'. Facial features are, of course, the surest way to distinguish the two genders, but once again, this is frequently disregarded in shoujo manga.

HOW TO DRAW MANGA

Drawing The Figure

As mentioned on the previous page, there are distinct differences between the male and female form, but the process is still the same. So, let's begin with the layout.

Follow step 1 from the male figure, remembering that the female torso tapers in the middle, giving the hourglass shape. Also, keep the limbs lean and curvy rather than thick and angular.

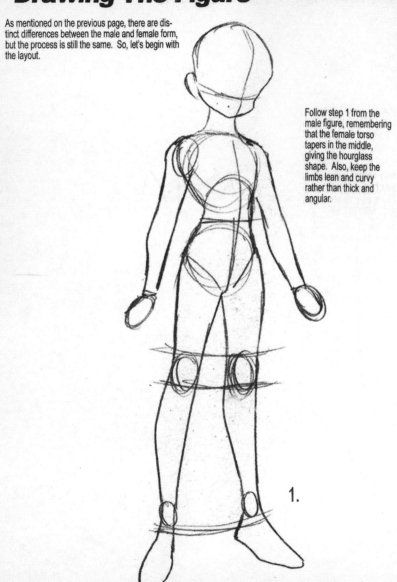

1.

Drawing The Figure

Again, using guide-
lines, layout the
facial features.
Giving the hint of
eyelashes is a great
way to add that
touch of femininity.
Using guidelines in
the chest will help
properly position the
breasts.

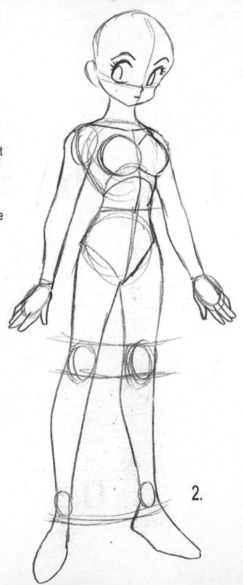

2.

Drawing The Figure

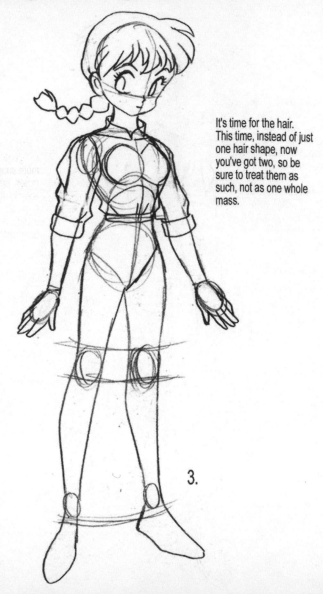

It's time for the hair. This time, instead of just one hair shape, now you've got two, so be sure to treat them as such, not as one whole mass.

3.

HOW TO DRAW MANGA

Drawing The Figure

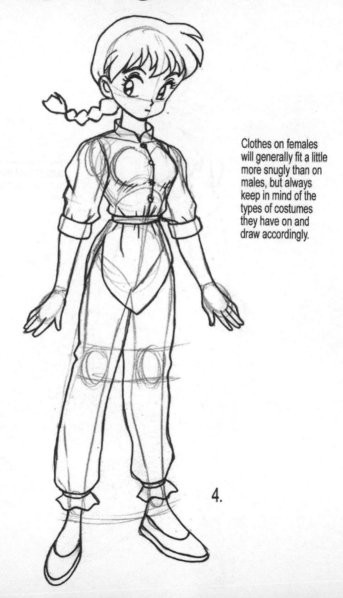

Clothes on females will generally fit a little more snugly than on males, but always keep in mind of the types of costumes they have on and draw accordingly.

4.

Drawing The Figure

Lay out your
shadows and
highlights in
pencil.

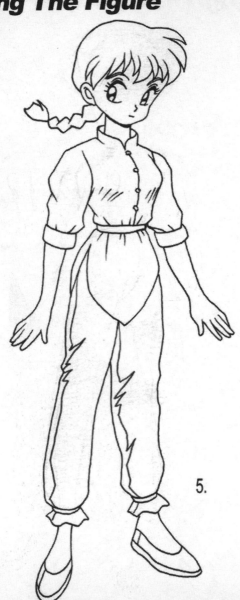

5.

HOW TO DRAW MANGA

Drawing The Figure

There is nothing wrong with emulating your favorite manga—in fact, I quite encourage it. In Japan, it is institutionally nurtured through the apprentice system, which has young artists working under the supervision of more experienced masters.

Ink and go!

6.

PRACTICE PAGE

Drawing The Figure

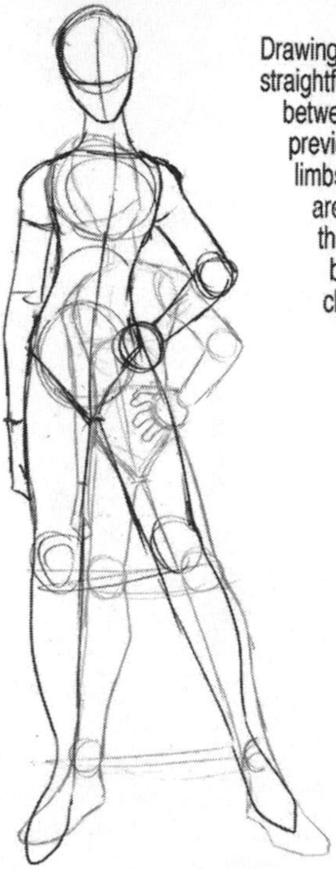

Drawing adult characters is fairly straightforward. The major difference between these figures and the previous younger ones is that their limbs are longer and their heads are slightly smaller. This makes them slightly more proportionally balanced than younger characters, probably since they have grown out of puberty.

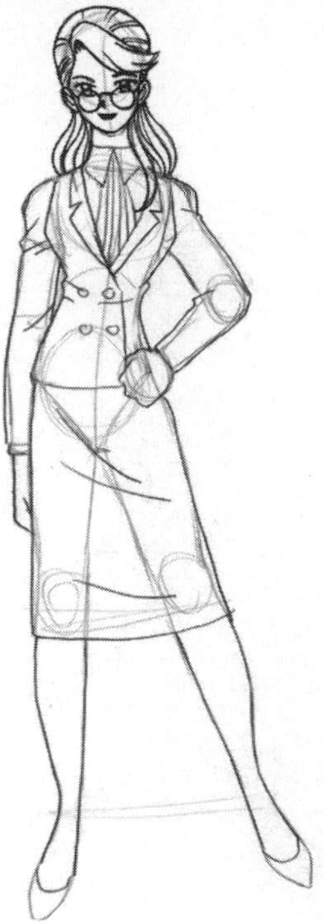

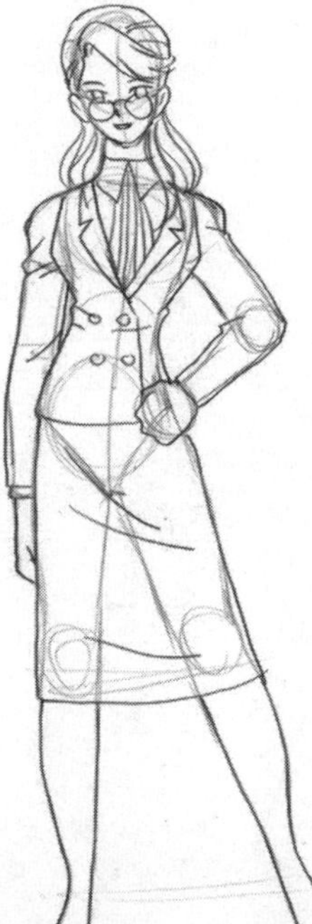

Drawing the Figure

Of course not every character you are going to draw will be a young, teen to twenty-something male or female. You may even want to create a manga aimed at a more mature audience, and then you will definitely need adult characters.

You will be pretty hard pressed to tell a story without any adults, although it has been done, so take the time to learn the small alterations you need to make to create believable adults. The same body differences between males and females still apply.

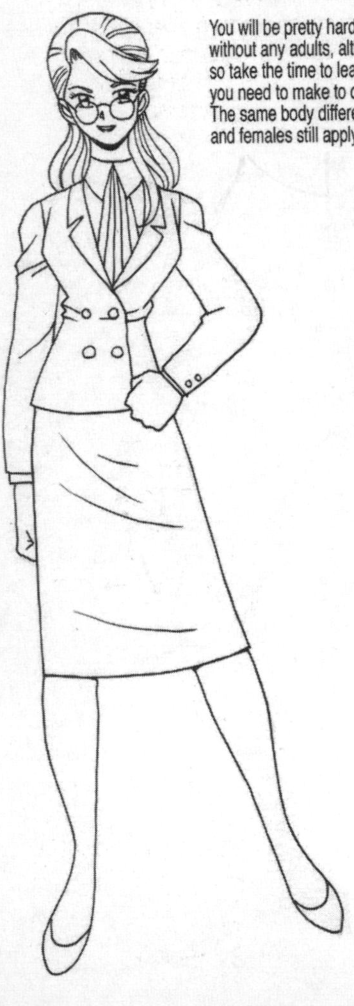

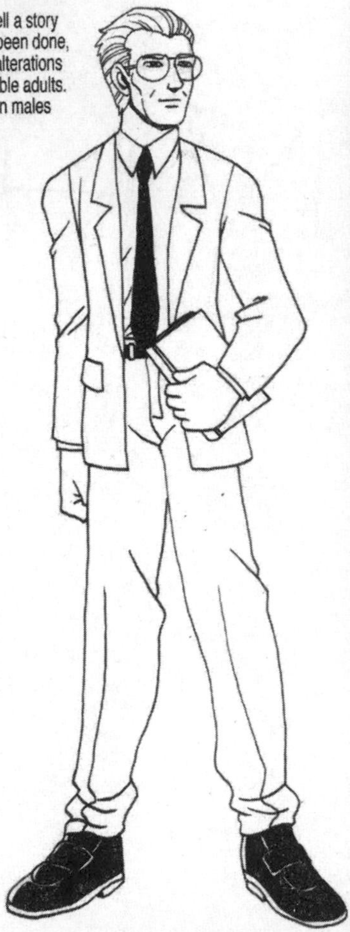

HOW TO DRAW MANGA

Drawing the Figure

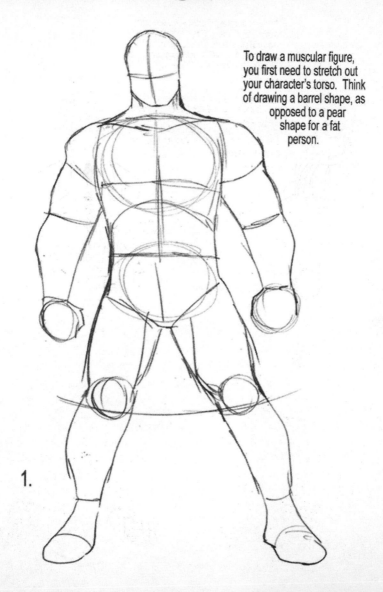

To draw a muscular figure, you first need to stretch out your character's torso. Think of drawing a barrel shape, as opposed to a pear shape for a fat person.

1.

Drawing the Figure

Then exaggerate all the muscles that you normally draw by broadening them.

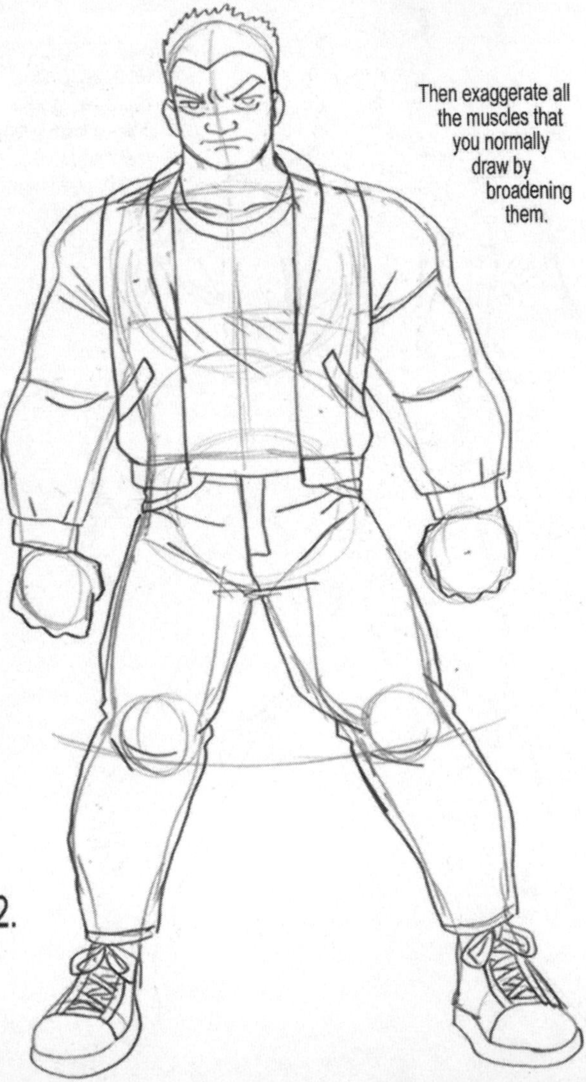

2.

HOW TO DRAW MANGA

Drawing the Figure

You can also make a character appear more muscular by drawing them in tight clothing.

3.

Drawing the Figure

In American comics, this is the most common body type, the muscular male. In manga, it is uncommon, and when it is used, you are almost always dealing with someone who is an antagonist, usually a bully.

Even in manga that revolve around hand-to-hand combat, the overly muscular form is not one that is idolized. Instead, the idealized male form in most manga is a body that has a balance between strength, flexibility and dexterity.

4.

PRACTICE PAGE

Drawing the Figure

Manga does an incredible job of reflecting reality and all its facets, and in the real world, not everyone is slim and trim. Even if none of your main characters are overweight, you will want to learn how to draw this body type so you can create variety in your background figures.

All the same figure-drawing rules apply, though since you are drawing an overweight person, the overweight body-shape will fall more into a pear shape than a rectangle.

HOW TO DRAW MANGA

Drawing the Figure

Remember that it is not enough to simply draw a large belly on a figure to make it fat.

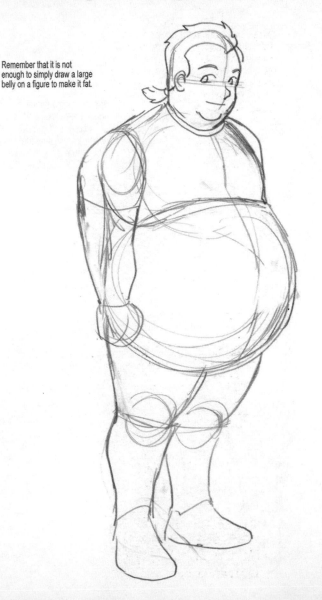

Drawing the Figure

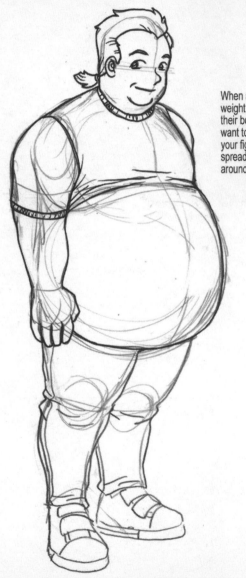

When a person gains weight, they gain it all over their body, and you will want to make sure that your figure is balanced by spreading the weight around evenly.

Drawing the Figure

Men and woman gain weight differently, with men tending to carry a lot of weight around their midriffs. In contrast, women often gain weight in their thighs and breasts as well as their midriffs. If you are not certain how a person will look, use reference. In fact, use reference as often as possible!

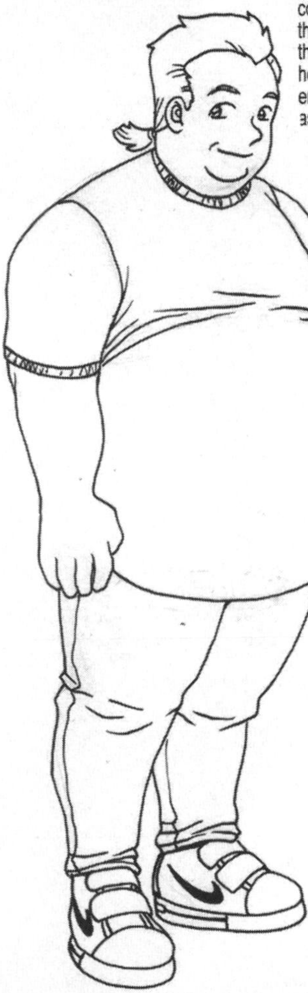

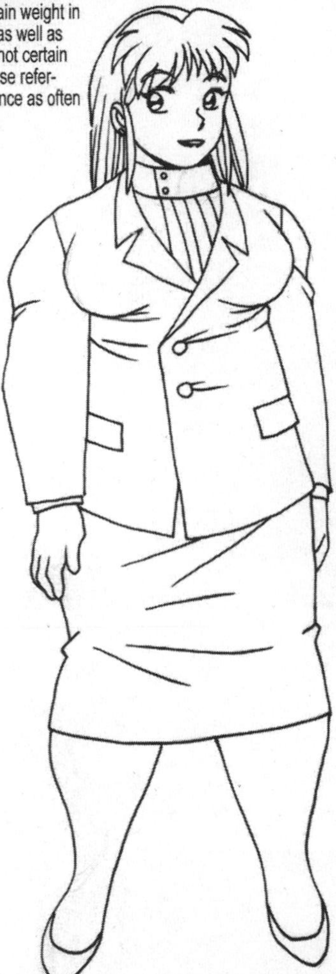

PRACTICE PAGE

Drawing the Figure

The old man may be the most versatile character in fantastic fiction. The archetype that immediately springs to mind the is lecherous old man, but there are so many others. The old man who sends the young heroes on a mission, the old man who leads the heroes on a quest, the patriarch of the family whom the hero is trying to please, and the curmudgeon with whom the hero has to put up are just a few of the examples of what this body type is used for, so I hope you have mastered it.

This body type is more slender or even wizened. Stoop the back over and bend all the limbs.

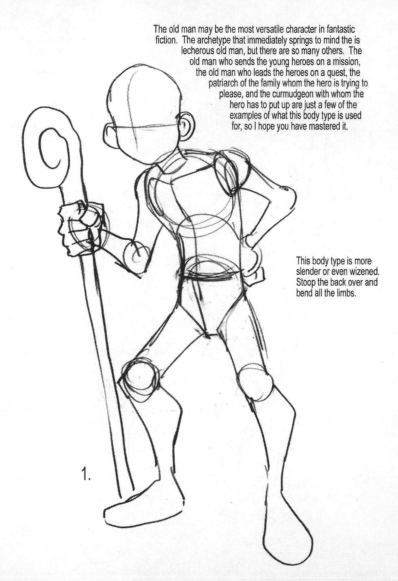

1.

Drawing the Figure

If you are going to lean an older man against a cane, make sure that you have enough bend in the arms and body to give the lean a sense of weight.

Drawing the Figure

Then go on and add some wrinkles. It can be as simple as
some lines on the forehead or as
involved as complex tracery all
over the face.

3.

HOW TO DRAW MANGA

Drawing the Figure

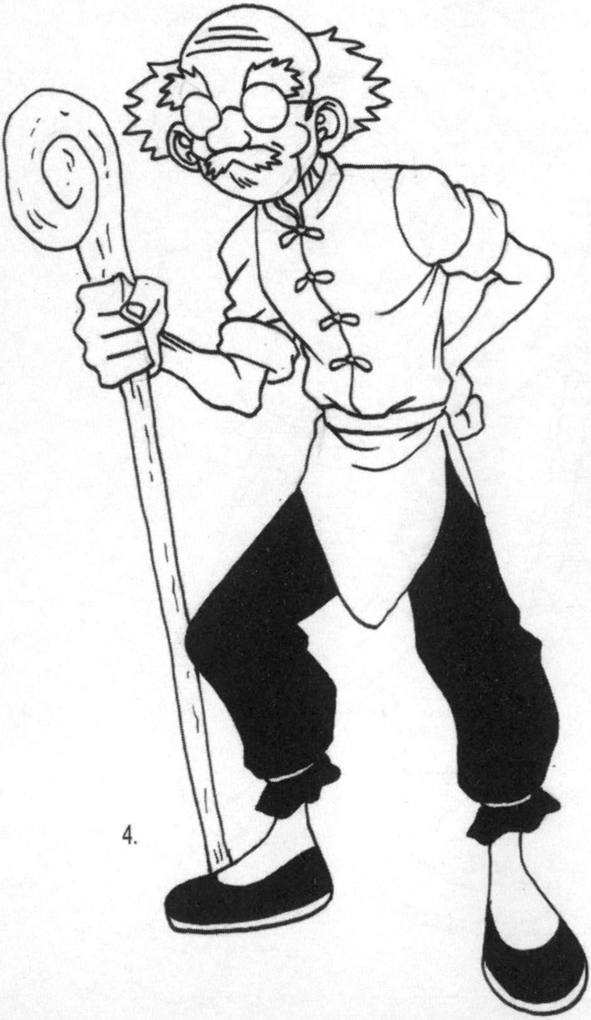

4.

PRACTICE PAGE

MASTER MANGA ON THE GO!

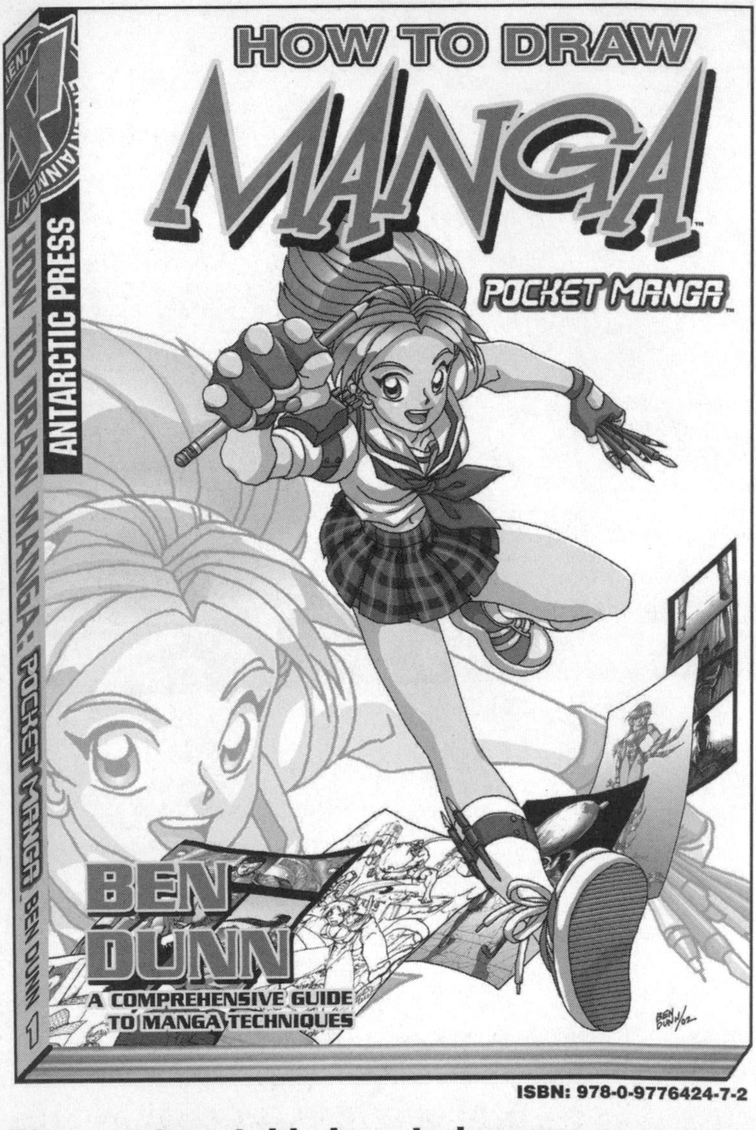
HOW TO DRAW
MANGA
POCKET MANGA
BEN DUNN
A COMPREHENSIVE GUIDE TO MANGA TECHNIQUES
ANTARCTIC PRESS
HOW TO DRAW MANGA: POCKET MANGA BEN DUNN 1

ISBN: 978-0-9776424-7-2

The most portable how-to lessons ever are now available for you to learn anywhere!

Pocket a purchase at your local comics or book retailer, or at www.antarctic-press.com!

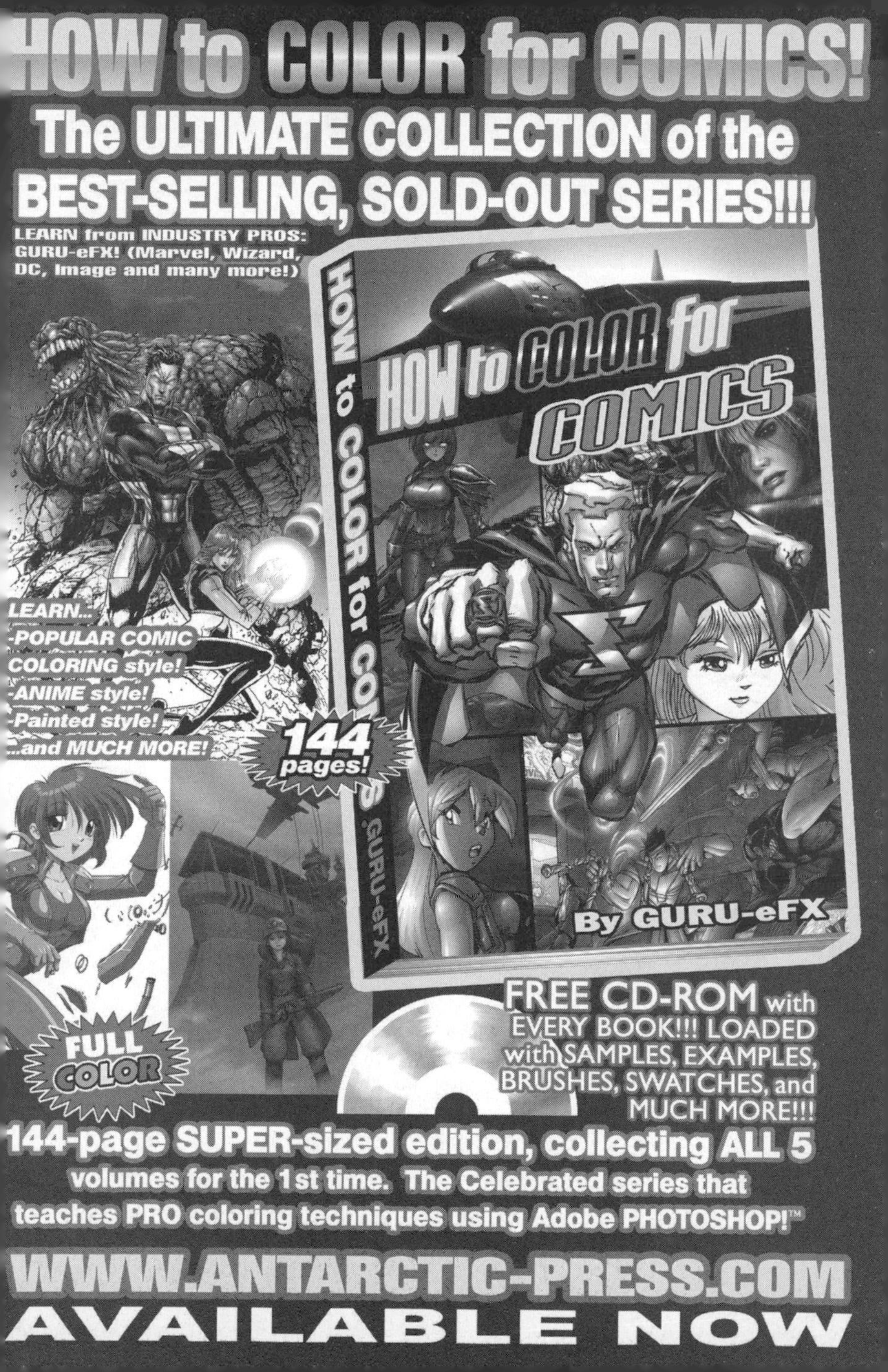
HOW to COLOR for COMICS!
The ULTIMATE COLLECTION of the
BEST-SELLING, SOLD-OUT SERIES!!!
LEARN from INDUSTRY PROS:
GURU-eFX! (Marvel, Wizard,
DC, Image and many more!)
HOW to COLOR for COMICS
HOW to COLOR for COMICS
GURU-eFX
By GURU-eFX
LEARN...
-POPULAR COMIC
COLORING style!
-ANIME style!
-Painted style!
...and MUCH MORE!
144 pages!
FULL COLOR
FREE CD-ROM with
EVERY BOOK!!! LOADED
with SAMPLES, EXAMPLES,
BRUSHES, SWATCHES, and
MUCH MORE!!!
144-page SUPER-sized edition, collecting ALL 5
volumes for the 1st time. The Celebrated series that
teaches PRO coloring techniques using Adobe PHOTOSHOP!™
WWW.ANTARCTIC-PRESS.COM
AVAILABLE NOW

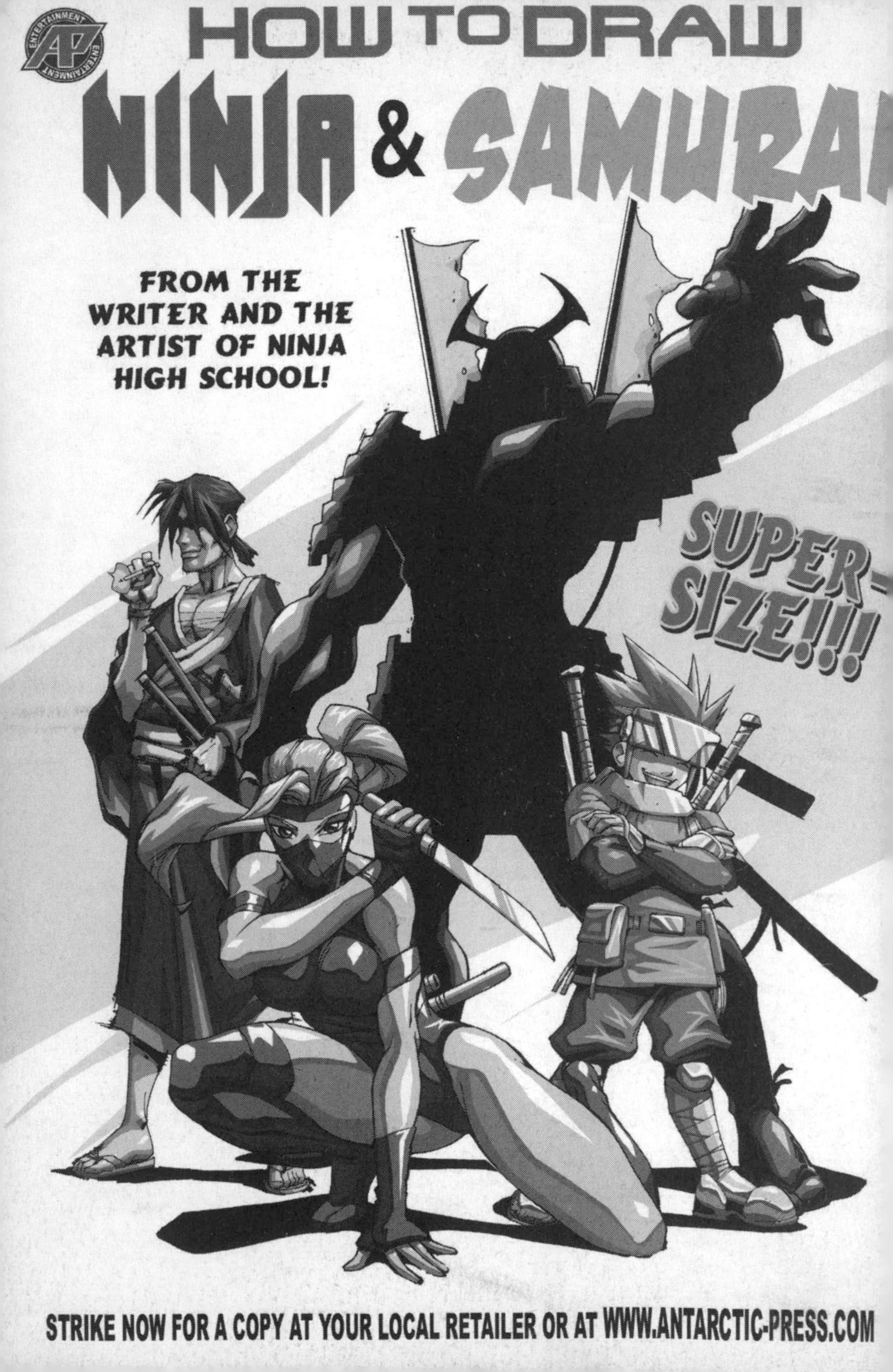
ENTERTAINMENT AP ENTERTAINMENT
HOW TO DRAW
NINJA & SAMURAI
FROM THE WRITER AND THE ARTIST OF NINJA HIGH SCHOOL!
SUPER-SIZE!!!
STRIKE NOW FOR A COPY AT YOUR LOCAL RETAILER OR AT WWW.ANTARCTIC-PRESS.COM

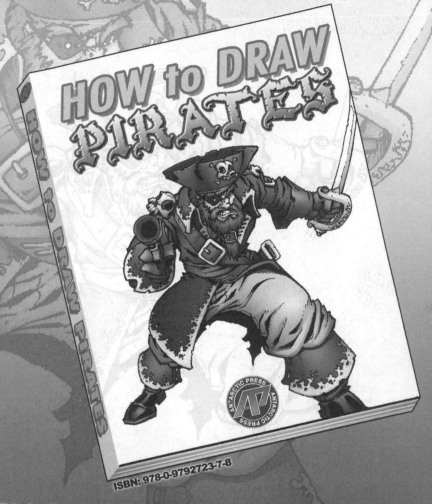